VW Beetle Restoration Handbook

How to Restore 1949–1967 VW Beetles to Original Factory Condition

From the Editors of *VW Trends* Magazine

HPBOOKS

HPBooks
are published by
The Berkley Publishing Group
A division of Penguin Putnam Inc.
375 Hudson Street
New York, New York 10014

First edition: June 2000

Library of Congress Cataloging-in-Publication Data

VW Beetle restoration handbook : how to restore 1949–1967 VW Beetles to original
factory condition / from the editors of *VW Trends* magazine—1st ed.
    p. cm.
    ISBN 1-55788-342-4
    1. Volkswagen Beetle automobile—Conservation and restoration. 2. Volkswagen Beetle
automobile—Customizing. I. *VW trends*.

TL215.V6 V8827 2000
629.28'722—dc21   00-027447

Book design and production by Michael Lutfy
Cover design by Bird Studios
Cover photo courtesy *VW Trends*

NOTICE: The information in this book is true and complete to the best of our knowledge. All recommendations on parts and procedures are made without any guarantees on the part of the author or the publisher. Tampering with, altering, modifying or removing any emissions-control device is a violation of federal law. Author and publisher disclaim all liability incurred in connection with the use of this information. The information contained herein was originally published in *VW Trends* magazine and is reprinted under license with McMullen Argus Publishing, 2400 E. Katella Ave., Anaheim, CA 92806. *VW Trends* is a registered trademark of McMullen Argus Publishers, Inc.

CONTENTS

ACKNOWLEDGMENTS

The publishers wish to gratefully acknowledge Craig Nickerson, Brian Van Mols, Ryan Lee Price, Robert Torrico, Dave Cormack and Sharon Malm for their contributions and support that have made the publication of this book possible. Other contributors include: Hank Roed, D.E. Meyer and Henry Z. DeKuyper.

Mechanically Minded vs. Mechanical

On a workbench in the back of my garage is an electric pencil sharpener that my wife Kara brought home from her classroom one day (she's an elementary school teacher). She told me that it didn't work anymore, and wondered if I could fix it. I smiled confidently at her silly question, and assured her that it would be sharpening with the best of them by the very next day.

Such is the essence of the male ego: we guys feel we can repair almost anything, even if we've never unscrewed a light bulb before. Just give us a set of tools, any tools, and we can fix anything. Just take it apart, put in some new parts, then screw the thing back together again—right? The first time I applied this theory, it was to a transistor radio with too much static, and now it doesn't work in a whole new way—it is now completely silent. The pencil sharpener soon suffered a similar fate, which was depressing.

I've always considered myself a mechanically minded person, but I guess I've just never been very mechanical—there is a difference. Extremely technical concepts come easy to me. Trigonometry, physics and engineering priniciples are no problem. I know the physical structure of an engine, and I understand the theory of internal combustion, but I could never see myself as someone who could tear an engine down, diagnosis the problem and put it back together again to make it work. My lack of confidence stems from my lack of actual hands-on experience.

Even when I was regularly driving my '71 Sedan, I would have been completely lost if something major had gone wrong, which eventually it did. I don't remember exactly what happened, but the engine made very loud, unusual noises, belched smoke and vibrated like an orbital polisher. My 30-second diagnosis was to replace the entire engine instead of trying to fix it. Maybe that was the best thing for the car at the time, but I'll never know, because I washed over the situation with a blanket solution. The easy way out.

But recently I crossed a major threshold in my life. I took apart something I knew nothing about, rebuilt it and put it back together again. And it wasn't something simple either; it was my carburetor, a device that has been known to confound even the most hard-core mechanic. Sure, a lot of you VW enthusiasts are saying, "That's easy, anybody can do that." For guys like you, maybe it is. However, I was afraid it would end up on the same list as the radio and pencil sharpener. This project was more intimidating than both of those, and I was about to revert to my old "have someone replace it" approach to mechanical repair, when I decided I'd had enough.

I forced myself to go out to the back of that car, pull out the carburetor and just fix the thing. I bought a rebuild kit from my local VW supply store, followed the directions included (which didn't really help much), and by the end of the weekend, I had a rebuilt carburetor that actually worked. I don't really care that it leaks a little gas at the throttle joint; it's functional, and the satisfaction of having done it myself is something that money just doesn't buy.

And therein lies the purpose of this book, which is to encourage you to jump right in and restore your vintage Beetle with your own two hands. It will give you an advantage that I didn't have, which is information and step-by-step photos to guide you through your project. If you have plenty of hands-on experience, then this book is merely a complementary guide. If you have little time under the hood, then it is a lifesaver. Perhaps, as you stand at the rear of an aircooled VW, wrench in hand and wondering where to start, this book will point the way and help increase your chances for success. It represents the best efforts of the best contributors and staff here at *VW Trends*. Good luck. —Ryan Lee Price, Editor, *VW Trends*

PORTING AND POLISHING SINGLE PORT HEADS

1

Text & Photography by Dave Cormack

As part of your routine maintenance, you should check valve clearances on your Bug's engine. It should read 0.004 inches between the valve stem and rocker arm. During one inspection, Dave Cormack, *VW Trends* Tech Editor, got through the number one exhaust and went on to the number one intake. As bad luck would have it, he couldn't get the feeler gauge in there. In fact, he couldn't get any feeler gauge in there. Hmmm—trouble.

So, the next step was to remove the adjusting screw from the rocker arm and see if maybe the keeper decided to part company with the valve stem. No such luck; as he removed the adjusting screw, the valve spring and retainer kept coming and coming. It finally hit the rocker arm on the lever part and bound up the pushrod. Not a good sign. The only good part was that he found this out in the comfort of his garage, not out on the highway somewhere.

The diagnosis was that he had dropped a valve seat. Out came the engine, and off came the heads, which were sent to Performance Technology, in Anaheim, CA, to see what Fred Simpson, along with crew Mike Di Giulio and Anthony Chicca. Fred is one of the foremost head builders in the industry, and some of the fastest VWs in the world are running Perf-Tech heads.

After inspection Fred, Mike and Anthony confirmed Dave's worst fears: The heads were too far gone, they were cracked, and they had been run loose. A new pair of single port heads was needed. While looking around for a new pair, Cormack asked Fred what he would recommend for a little more performance. He thought about it a while and came up with an idea. Why not do a port and polish, and install a set of 40mm x 37.5mm stainless steel valves? This would not only give a little more pep, but should increase the efficiency, thereby decreasing the engine temperature and increasing the gas mileage. Let's follow along as Fred works his magic on the new set of single ports. By the way, when was the last time you saw a new set of single port heads?

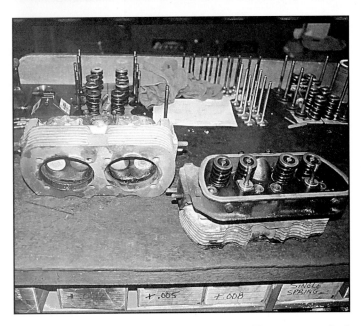

1. Here is the broken set of single port heads. They were cracked between the valve seats and the spark plug hole; they had been run loose and probably just plain seen better days.

2. To install the new nickel/chromium oversize valve seats the heads needed to be cut. Once the hole is large enough, the heads are put into an oven and heated to 400 degrees, then left in the oven for about an hour.

3. Mike installs the seats into the new head. Although you can't tell from the photographs, you could get a two-minute egg in about 30 seconds on these heads; they were *hot*. Fred uses a .008-inch interference fit to make sure the seats stay put.

4. Here is a shot of the head with all four valve seats in. They will be cut for the BugPack stainless steel valves after the rest of the work is performed.

5. Here Fred is beginning to polish the exhaust port. As you can tell from the lead photo, he also went after the intake ports, too.

6. Here's a good shot of some of Fred's handiwork. The intake and exhaust ports are ported and polished, and ready for the valve guides to be installed.

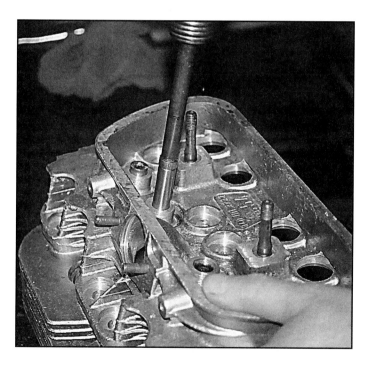

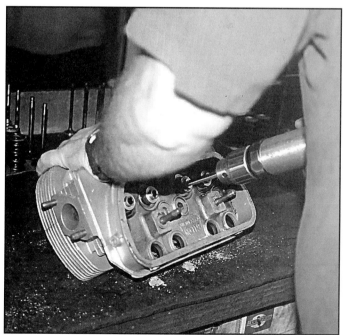

7. Fred installs the guides using a pneumatic hammer with a pilot shaft to hold the guide.

8. Now the guides are reamed to fit the 8mm stem diameter of the BugPack stainless steel valves.

9. The intake ports received the Simpson treatment also. If you aren't making the aluminum fly, you aren't porting the heads.

10. The seats are now cut for the 40mm x 37.5mm valves.

11. At the bottom of the valve seats you will see a lip that needs to be smoothed out for maximum airflow.

12. These are the valves we will be using. They are made of stainless steel, so we can run unleaded fuel.

13. Fred is shown here lapping the valves to the seats the old-fashioned way: by hand.

14. Now the shims, springs, retainers and keepers are installed. Fred has an air-powered valve spring compressor that makes the job a breeze.

15. Here is the finished product, ready to install.

SOURCE BOX

Performance Technology
1631 Placentia, Unit "M"
Anaheim, CA 92805
Tel: (714) 526-0533
Fax: (714) 526-1366
www.racingheads.com

BugPack Products
3560 Cadillac Avenue
Costa Mesa, CA 92626
(714) 979-4990
fax: (714) 979-3468
www.BUGPACK.com

2 ADJUSTING VALVES

Text & Photography by Dave Cormack

1. The first thing to do is to take a screwdriver and pry off the two clips that hold the distributor cap onto the distributor. Let the cap rest somewhere where it won't be in the way when you manually turn the engine over.

While the subject may be redundant to some of you who have long been adjusting your own valves, there are some of our readers who are just getting into this hobby. There are also some people who still send their cars to a mechanic for the required valve adjustment that is supposed to occur every 3,000 miles.

It's not that hard to do and requires a minimum number of tools. A shop rag, a set of valve cover gaskets, a feeler gauge with 0.004 in. gauge, a 13mm open-end or box-end wrench, a screwdriver and a crescent wrench are all that you need to set your own valves. The first time you do it might take about an hour, but once you get used to the procedure, it will take only 20 minutes or so.

The first thing to do is to place the car where you will be working on it the night before you actually take a wrench to it. This is to ensure that the valves will be cold. Back in the late 1960s, Volkswagen issued a bulletin saying that the valves could be set when the temperature was below 50 degrees centigrade (122 degrees Fahrenheit). They would put a blower on the engine to bring it down to the required temperature. I have always done it the old-fashioned way, with the valves dead cold, and that's how I'm going to show you how to do it.

Now, the first thing in the morning, after you've had your coffee, or whatever, wander out to your car, chock the wheels, set the parking brake and put the car into neutral. Open up the decklid, and prop it up if your decklid spring doesn't hold the decklid up, or you are using decklid standoffs. Baja and buggy people obviously don't have to worry about this.

If you don't have an aluminum degree pulley and your crankshaft pulley isn't marked, you will have to mark TDC (Top Dead Center), and also 180 degrees from Top Dead Center (BDC, or Bottom Dead Center).

2. & 2a. Grab a crescent wrench and turn the engine over in the direction that it goes when it's running. Look for the notches in the crank pulley on the side of the pulley that is closest to the engine. You may have one, two or three notches. As you turn the engine in the rotation that it goes when it is running, line the last notch up with the crack that separates the case halves. Also, look at the rim of the distributor body; you will see a notch in the rim. The rotor should be pointing at the notch in the rim. If it isn't, turn the engine another 360 degrees until the rotor is pointed at the notch in the rim of the distributor body, still lining up the last notch in the crank pulley with the seam for the case halves. Put a dab of paint, or fingernail polish, or whatever, on the notch, and then do the same directly below the other paint mark, 180 degrees from where the first mark is. Aluminum degree wheel people don't need to do this; just make sure the rotor is pointed to the notch on the rim of the distributor, and the pulley says "TDC" at the case seam.

3. Take a shop rag and thread it through the valve cover bail. Pull out and down on the rag and make the valve cover bail comes down to the bottom portion of the head. Lift the valve cover off, bearing in mind that there will probably be some oil that will come out of the head. I usually lay the valve cover directly underneath the head to catch the oil dripping from the head.

4. This is what you should see. We will be adjusting number one exhaust and intake valve first, as this is where we have the engine set.

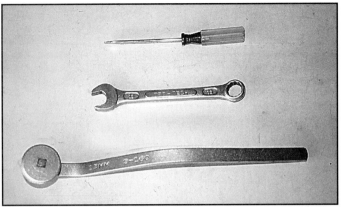

5. There are a number of different tools made specifically for the purpose of adjusting the valves; this one (bottom of photo) is made by Mac Tools. A number of our advertisers carry tools similar to this that perform the same function, but they are not necessary; they just make the job a little easier. For the home mechanic, however, a 13mm open-end wrench or box-end wrench and a flat blade screwdriver will do.

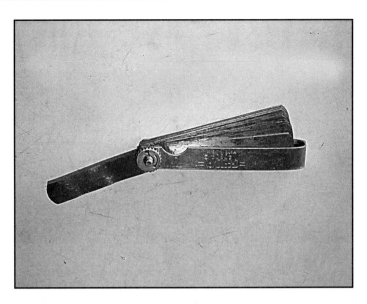

6. The 0.004" feeler gauge shown has seen better days and should be replaced for an accurate measurement.

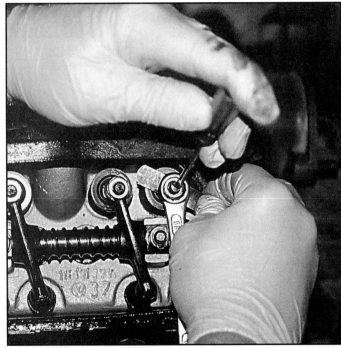

7. We will begin by trying the 0.004" feeler gauge on number one exhaust valve. This is the one on the passenger side, closest to the front of the car. Start by trying to stick the 0.004" feeler gauge between the rocker arm and the stem of the valve. If it will fit and there is only a slight amount of drag on the feeler gauge, then you don't need to set that particular valve. If it goes through loosely, or won't fit in at all, then you will need to set it. If the valve clearance needs adjusting, take your 13mm wrench and loosen up the lock nut on the top of the rocker arm. Open up the clearance by turning the adjusting screw out and inserting the feeler gauge in. Turn the adjusting screw until there is a slight drag on the feeler gauge, then tighten down the lock nut. Recheck the clearance, as the adjusting screw has a tendency to turn when the lock nut is tightened. Do it until you are sure it is right.

8. Now that you are happy with number one exhaust, move on to the number one intake valve, which is the next one back, toward the back of the car. Repeat the process you just used on number one exhaust.

9. Now that number one cylinder is adjusted, grab the crescent wrench, and turn the engine 180 degrees opposite the way it runs (backwards), to the mark you made that is opposite of the timing marks, which are the notches on the crank pulley. Aluminum degree people just move the engine backwards until the letters "BDC" line up with the case half seam.

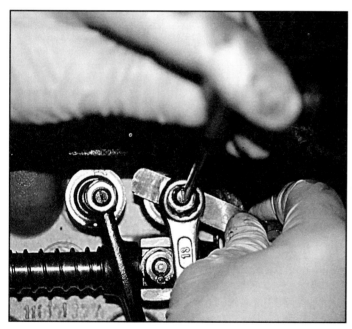

10. Now you are ready to do the same thing on number two intake and exhaust valves. When done, turn the engine backwards again, until the notch in the crank pulley is lined up with the split in the case halves. Replace the valve cover gasket with a new one, making sure the sealing surfaces of both the valve cover and the cylinder head are clean and free from any pieces of old gasket, sealer, etc. Also, if you wish to use a sealer, put it on the valve cover side of the gasket, never on the cylinder head. Go to the other side of the car, remove the valve cover and repeat this procedure on number three cylinder, which comprises the two valves closest to the front of the car. Once again, aluminum degree pulley people will be back at "TDC."

11. When you are done with number three cylinder, turn the engine backwards 180 degrees again, (aluminum—"BDC") and set the clearance on number four cylinder, which will be the only two you haven't touched yet. When you are done with number four cylinder, replace the valve cover and gasket on that side, put the distributor cap back on, clean up and you're done. Now, that wasn't so hard, was it? With the prices charged nowadays for a valve adjustment, you can save enough money by doing your own adjustments that you will very soon recoup the money spent on the tools you need.

3 ETHAN'S RIDE

by Karl Funke: Photography by Henry Z. DeKuyper

Nelson Huckeba, of Grand Prairie, Texas, is another one of those extremely devoted guys who has been into the VW scene since he was first able to drive. Back when Nelson was 16 his brother, Lee, passed his '66 Baja to his younger brother, and thus kindling Nelson's interest in vintage VWs at an early age; since that first Bug, Nelson has owned two others, a Beetle and a Baja, from 1964 and 1969 respectively. Nelson purchased the car, a 1965 Beetle, in hopes of building the perfect show-quality daily driver. When he bought the car, it was in original condition and rust free to boot; the folks he got it from were the original owners. Once he had

end was completely redone, with new king and link pins and grease seals, and virtually every part of the brake assembly was replaced and/or detailed. The front trailing arms, pitman arm, and other various brake parts were originally powdercoated grey, but were later color matched to the body.

The rest of the pan, including the axle tubes, spring plates, spindles, drums, was powdercoated in Porsche red. CB Performance dropped spindles and a BugPack dropped beam were added as well, lowering this Bug 3 inches in back and a low, low 6-1/2 inches up front. Shock absorption comes courtesy of KYB on all four corners. Wheels are stock 15 inchers wrapped with Camac 135s on front and 165s in

it home, he proceeded to strip the Bug of all parts, wires, nuts and bolts. The body was taken off the pan, and Nelson worked for the next week removing all the exterior paint, including the fender wells and engine compartment, until the whole thing was stripped to bare metal. The body was then towed on a donated '57 pan to his friend Patrick Askin in Winnfield, La., where the body work and painting would take place. Nelson kept the '65 pan and started work on it himself.

He tore down the pan, cleaned off the tar board, then took it and all its pieces to Able's in Dallas, Texas, to be sandblasted. The front

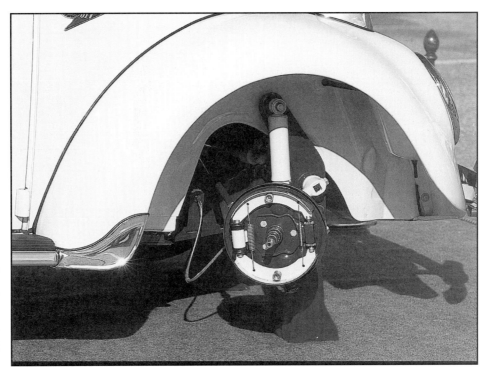

faulty brake fluid reservoir prevented him from driving it in; since Nelson built this car to drive, he had no intention of towing it. Nelson made it to his first show in May of 1996, but by then, he says, the car was a little chipped up by roughly 6000 miles of daily driving abuse. In February 1997, Nelson pulled the body off again and proceeded to detail the transmission, shocks, brake parts, master cylinder, tie rod ends, steering box, trailing arms, fender wells and the underside of the body in the same pearl white as the exterior.

back. Once he had the pan sorted out and put back together, he waited for Patrick to bring the body back to him.

The body came back eight days before the '95 Big Bug Shootout in Ennis, Texas. Patrick had performed all necessary body work, as well as spraying the four base coats of Centauri pearl white. Some of the more conspicuous additions to the exterior are Brazilian wide trim running boards from West Coast Metric, Blade Baby overriders on the front and rear bumpers, front and rear gravel guards, and side mirrors, also from West Coast Metric. Nelson worked feverishly to get the car back together in time for the upcoming show, but at the very last minute a

The Bug's engine was rebuilt by Scott Easdon of V-Dub Folks in Irving, Texas. The 90.5mm bore and 78mm stroke effect with a 2007cc displacement from the stock 1600. Rabbit rods swing from a stock crankshaft that has been

welded and reground with Rabbit journals. Stock solid shaft rockers shake inside polished chrome valve covers; the valves themselves are 39mm on the intake and 32mm on the exhaust. A heavy-duty oil pump keeps the lubrication flowing, and a Doghouse oil cooler keeps it cool. Exhaust consists of a BugPack 1-5/8 inch header and a Turbo Hideaway muffler. Ignition is handled by an all-Bosch setup (except for the wires, which are Empi 8mm), including an 009 distributor, Bosch blue coil, and Bosch Platinum plugs. The horses reach the pavement via a stock '65 swing axle transmission. Shifting is accomplished by way of a stock 200mm clutch disc, KEP1700-lb pressure plate, and a Scat Dragfast shifter.

The interior was redone through the combined efforts of several people. The seats are stock lowbacks covered by grey vinyl with tweed inserts; door panels are covered with the same. The carpet kit is charcoal grey loop from Sewfine, while the headliner is white perforated vinyl (installed by Preston's in Irving, Texas). The stock wiring loom was reinstalled by Kerry Woolsey. The dash remains stock, but sports a few custom goodies such as the West Coast Metrics knobs and grab handle and the bud vase from Koch's. The gauges are VDO stock, and the stereo is the original 1965 AM radio that came with the car.

Since the car has been done, Nelson has gotten some exposure at shows in his area—including the Texas Bug-In in Ennis and the Bugtoberfest in San Antonio. He has done quite well, winning numerous awards, including six first places. And, we're sure there are more to come.

INSTALLING POWER WINDOWS & DOOR LOCKS

4

Text & Photography by Dave Cormack

1. Here is the door, waiting for the crew at All German Auto to work their magic.

As most of you know, the Volkswagen Beetle was never meant to be a car that placed you in the lap of luxury. The very name means "people's car," a car for the masses, one that everyone could drive and enjoy. This was a no-frills car, one that had none of the amenities of the other, more luxurious cars of the time. And today, well, let's face it, the Beetle design is somewhat outdated by all of the technological improvements made over the last 20 years.

Most cars nowadays—at least all the cars that are above bargain-basement pricing—have power windows and door locks. We decided to see if there was any way we could update the old Beetle with these power windows, and, while we were at it, upgrade the door locks so that when you use the key to open the door, the passenger side locks and unlocks simultaneously, as in today's cars.

We made a call to Auto-Loc, in Hillsboro, Ore., to see if they could help us out. We had Auto-Loc send us its power window and door lock kit, and went to its authorized installer, All German Auto, in Escondido, Calif.,

where Sean Eves installed the kit on Adam Wood's 1967 Beetle.

A word of caution here: If you are not an accomplished spark-chaser, and don't have some fabricating skills, this might be a job better off left to the professionals. It can be done at home, however, if you have the time and patience to do it right. There are a lot of wires that need to be hooked up correctly the first time, or you will run the risk of damaging the existing wiring in your car, or the power window and door lock units, or all three. Now that I've said that, let's watch as Sean puts the Auto-Loc windows and door locks into Adam's '67.

Once again, I must reiterate: This is not a one- or two-hour job and not for the inexperienced enthusiast. The door locks and window assemblies are very well made, but they do require some expertise to install them correctly. If you think that this might be a little too complicated for you, call Auto-Loc and find an authorized installer near you. This is a very well-made kit, and should give years of trouble-free service.

2. The Auto-Loc kits come with just about everything you will need to perform the installation. This power window kit will fit a number of different cars; thus, some of the parts included will not be needed.

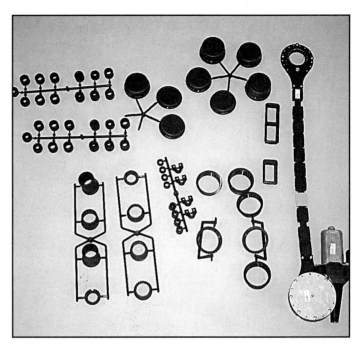

3. The first things that we did were lay out all of the parts in the kit, familiarize ourselves with all the pieces and parts and study the instructions. There is a lot of wiring involved in this kit so we wanted to make sure we had a good idea of what was going to go where before we started.

4. & 4a. We started the installation by taking off the inside door pulls and removing the roll pin from the window winder handle.

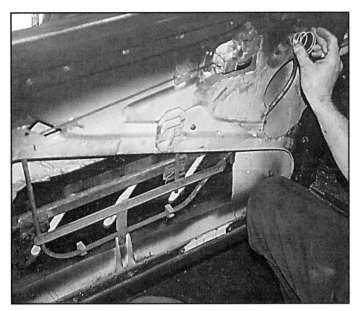

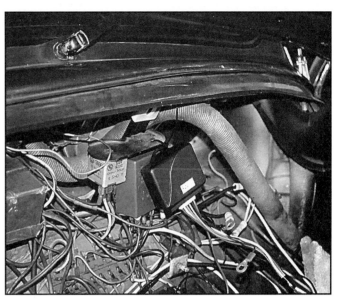

5. Then we took the door panels off, carefully so we don't scratch any paint. A wide-tipped spatula wrapped in a rag comes in handy here. The nice thing about using a 1965-and-later Beetle is that we already have the later-style window regulators in place. You can do the power window install with the earlier regulators too, however.

6. Here is what we are starting with. Now comes the wiring aspect of the installation. Sean routes all of the wires where they need to go first, then clips off the excess.

7. Sean ran all of the wires for the door locks under the cowl, over the top of the existing wiring and over the glovebox, for a clean installation that will be hard to see when the dash cover is put back on.

8. Sean used shrink-wrap to encase the wires, once he figured out where all of them go. He also opted to run two harnesses on the driver's side, as he felt that the wiring for both the power windows and the door locks would be too thick for the door seal, which could possibly crush the wires when the door is closed, leading to problems later on.

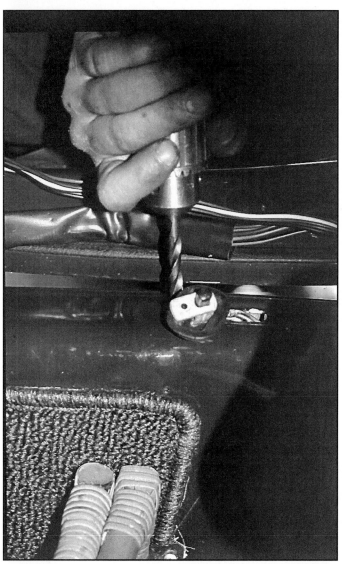

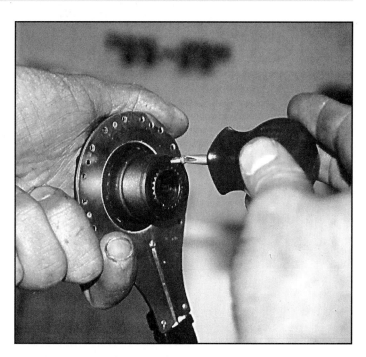

10. Sean determined which set of gears would work for our application. There will be three gears stacked onto each other, in order to mate the motor to our splined window winder shaft.

9. You do have to drill a few small holes into the door, and also the "A" pillar, but they are pretty small in diameter, so you could easily plug them if you ever wanted to go back to the stock wind up windows.

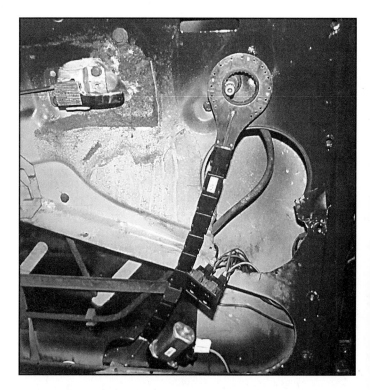

11. Now we begin placement of the motor and cable unit. We put it at the bottom of the door, so that we wouldn't have any more bends in the cable housing than absolutely necessary. They are designed to work in just about any angle and configuration, however.

12. & 12a. There are some braces that need to be installed on the inner door skin to prevent flexing when the motor is actuated. Sean figures out the best placement and then cuts and trims the braces to fit.

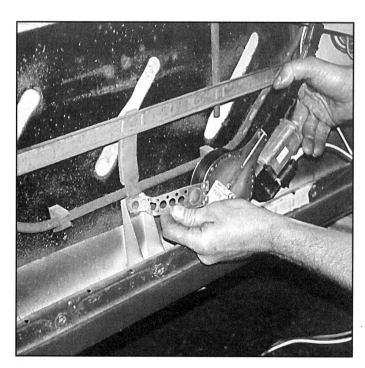

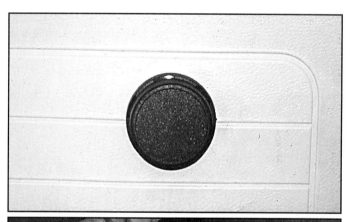
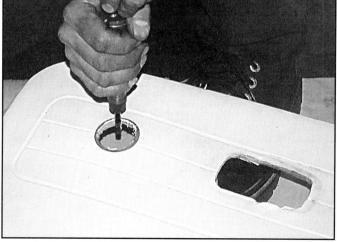

13. Sean mounts the motor down inside the door, keeping it away from the regulator, and mounting it securely to avoid flex when the windows are rolled up and down.

14. & 14a. There are decorative plugs provided with the kit that cover the winder shaft. The door panels must be trimmed slightly to fit these in.

15. The switches also need to be mounted on the door panel, with two of them going on the driver's side, so the driver can control the passenger side window also. We mounted these close to the factory speaker or access hole, so we wouldn't have to cut any metal from the inner door skin. The door panels need to have a hole put in them for the switches also. Be careful, and measure twice, cut once!

16. Now Sean moves on to the wiring. He determines where everything is going to go and clips any extra wire that won't be needed.

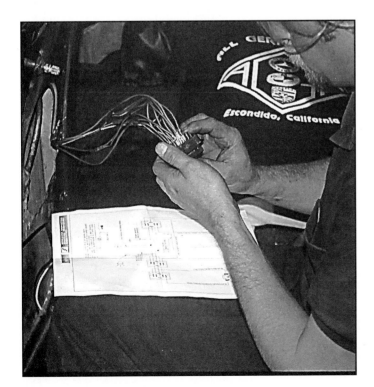

17. Sean now connects all the wiring, tests the windows and then moves on to the next phase of the project.

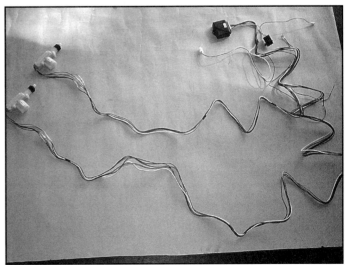

18. The power lock assemblies are next on the list. They are fairly simple to install, once you know where the solenoids are going to go in the door and have the wiring routed through the door, "A" pillar and across the dash to the passenger side.

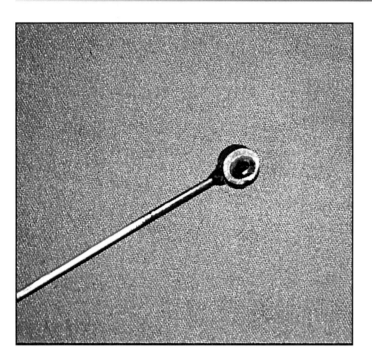

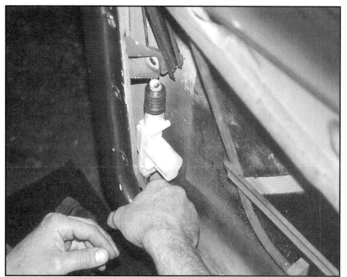

19. Martin Christensen, of All German Auto, made attaching the end of the door lock rod an easy job by fabricating this little rubber-insulated catch that just slides onto the pin on the lock mechanism. This is one of the things that needs to be done on this kit as one style of end will not fit every kind of car. The rubber insulation gives a nice, solid sound when the locks are opened or closed.

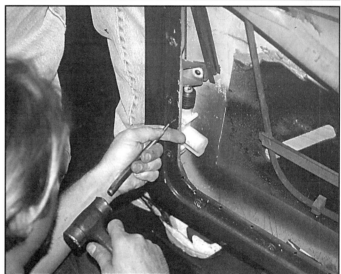

Auto-Loc
1281 NE 25th Street, Suite M, Dept. VWT
Hillsboro, OR, 97124
(800) 873-4038
www.autoloc.com

All German Auto
1327 Simpson Way, Dept. VWT
Escondido, CA, 92029
Tel: (760) 738-4626
Fax: (760) 738-8013

20., 20a., & 20b. Sean now moves on to installing the door lock solenoids. They must be correctly positioned so they work properly and then mounted into the inner door. Once again—measure twice (or three times) and cut once!

21. The wiring has already been positioned for the solenoids, so now it is a matter of bolting the solenoids in and connecting up the wiring as per the supplied Auto-Loc diagram.

22. This is what we have so far. Everything is compact and quite sturdy. This is a well-made kit, and I could find no quality problems. Other than having to fabricate a few little parts, which was anticipated because of the different applications associated with the kit, it went together with relatively little trouble. Of course, it helped that Sean and Martin are fabricators.

23. Adam installs his dash cover and gets ready to drive home with modern power and convenience. Notice the shirt Adam is wearing, too.

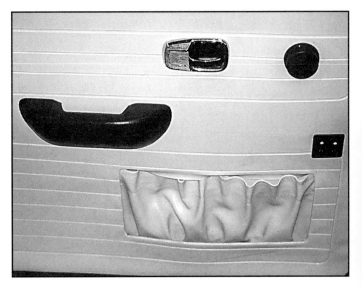

24. Now about all that was left was to reinstall the door panels after the final wiring and clean the panels with some vinyl cleaner to get all the grease and dirt off.

INSTALLING A BERG HARD-START SOLENOID

5

Text & Photography by Dave Cormack

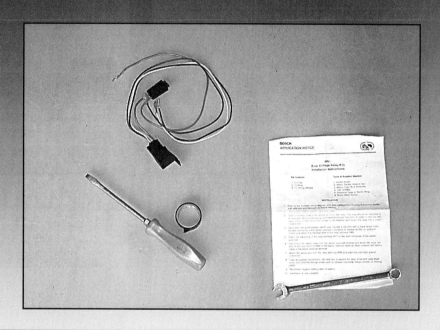

1. This is the Gene Berg hard-start solenoid kit. The only tools you need are the 13mm wrench to take the nut off the cable going to the starter, a drill and a screwdriver.

For the most part, the electrical system on the aircooled Volkswagen was a wonder of simplicity and reliability. As it was a basic, no-frills car, there wasn't a lot of wiring, solenoids, capacitors and electrical doo-dads involved.

One problem concerns starting, though. The way the electrical system is laid out, the starter gets its power from the switch. This means that, as the switch is turned, the current goes from the switch to the battery, back to the switch and then to the starter. This roundabout current flow can result in voltage loss and hard starting as the car gets older and corrosion of the wires and terminals takes its toll. There can be other reasons, too, of course, like a weak battery, bad starter or worn starter bushing, an ignition switch that is dirty or corroded or just plain worn out or other reasons. There is a simple fix to re-route the current path, however. Gene Berg Enterprises sells these hard-start solenoids that are easy to install and can make hard starting a thing of the past.

The whole operation took less than half an hour, it's

that simple. If you are having problems with hard starting of your car, this tech procedure could provide some help.

SOURCE

Gene Berg Enterprises
1725 North Lime Street
Orange, CA 92665
Tel: (714) 998-7500
Fax: (714) 998-7528
www.geneberg.com

23

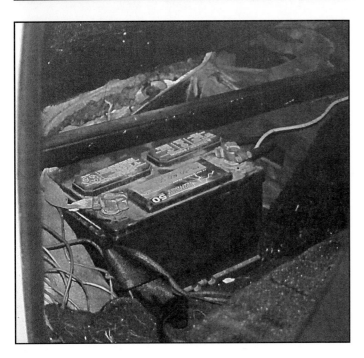

2. The first thing to do, as when working on any electrical part, is to disconnect the battery.

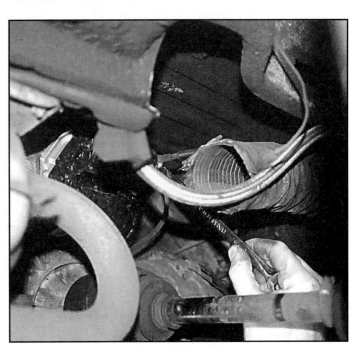

3. Disconnect the big cable coming from the battery to the starter. Also, remove the smaller wire; it is a push-on connector.

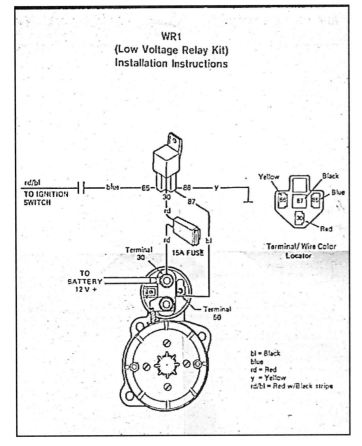

4. The wiring diagram supplied by Gene Berg is pretty much fool-proof. If you can read, you should have no trouble hooking this little unit up.

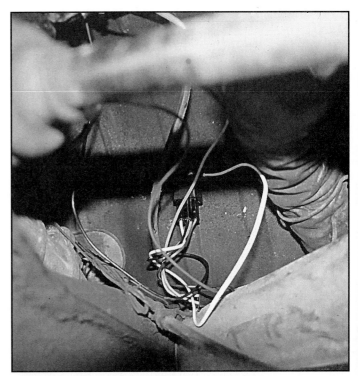

5. Mark mounted the solenoid for his car on the body, right in front of the starter itself. The closer to the starter you can have the wires, the less voltage drop you will have.

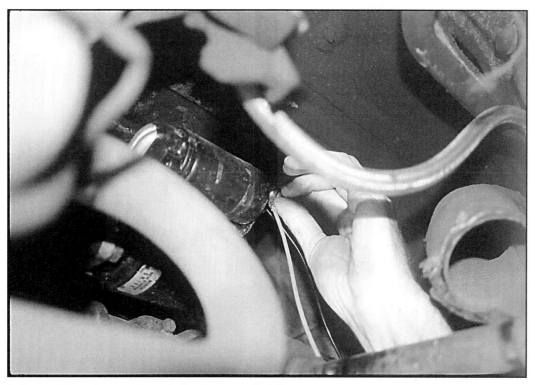

6. Connect the wires as shown in the Berg-supplied diagram.

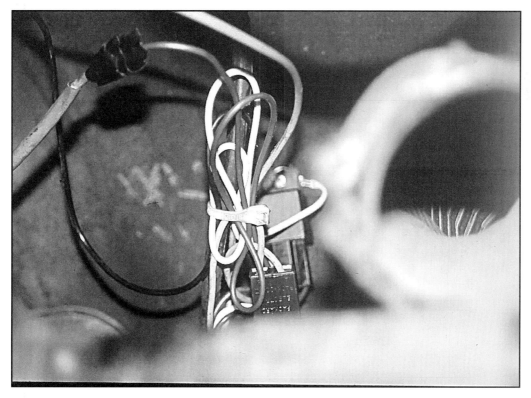

7. Mark used a couple of plastic tie-wraps to keep the wires together. When he has more time, he plans on shortening the wires and making a cleaner installation.

6 REPLACING THE IGNITION SWITCH

Text & Photography by Dave Cormack

1. Here we go. Begin by prying off the horn button. Be careful: These were made out of plastic, and will break easily.

The other day, an art director at one of *VW Trends'* sister publications mentioned that her 1970 Beetle Convertible was not starting, and needed to be pushed to get it started. We took the ailing Beetle over to Rhoads Enterprises in Stanton, Calif., where shop owner Dave Rhoads quickly diagnosed the problem as a faulty ignition switch. He jumped across the terminals at the starter, and the car started. Then, he went up to the switch, and jumped across the wires there. And he got nada. Okay, let's replace the switch. Now, in the old days, it was a simple matter to unscrew the fastener under the dash, unscrew the wires from the bad switch and install the new one. But with the advent of the switch being placed in the steering column, along with the locking steering wheel feature, things got a little more complicated. We watched Dave put a new switch in, and it only took about an hour's time.

2. Using a screwdriver, remove the three screws that hold the horn ring.

3. Using a 1/2-inch drive socket, remove the nut that holds the steering wheel in place.

4. Remove the steering wheel. Sometimes it is necessary to use a puller, because the wheel has been on for so long it refuses to come off without mechanical help. We got lucky, and the wheel came off easily by hand.

5. Remove the screws that hold the turn signal switch in place. Move the switch out of the way; it doesn't have to be removed entirely, just moved so that you can get to the switch cover screws.

6. Remove the screws for the ignition switch cover.

7. Pull the switch out enough to see all of the barrel portion. As you can tell, someone has been in here before, and did a not-so-good repair job, as evidenced by the patched wiring.

8. By removing this small screw on the bottom side of the switch holder, the switch will be separated from the switch holder.

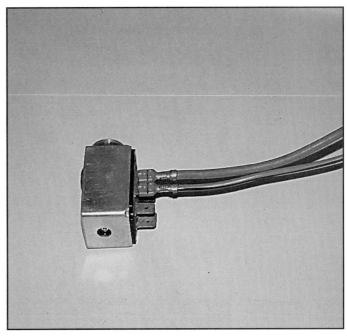

9. Here is the new switch, available from many VW parts suppliers.

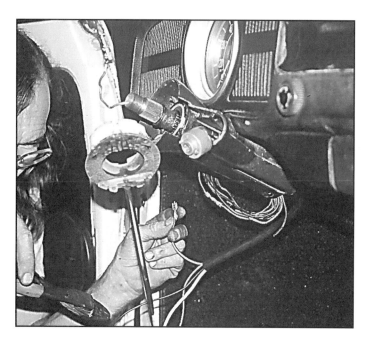

10. & 10a. Route the wire for the new switch through the column.

11. Once you have the wires through the column, it is a fairly simple task to put the new wires where the old ones were, take the old switch out and reassemble the turn signal switch, steering wheel, and horn ring and button. That's all there is to it; you should be able to accomplish this in about an hour's time. And it sure beats push-starting the car every time you need to go somewhere.

Rhoads Enterprises
8376 Katella Ave.
Stanton, CA 90680
(714) 952-2597

7 AN ALL-ORIGINAL '66 SUNROOF SEDAN

by Chris Mangler: Photography by Henry Z. DeKuyper

VW enthusiasts, it seems, are psychologically built to be opportunist—and who can blame them? Because when that sweet Volkswagen comes knocking on your door, you've just got to answer. Michael Grishman of Berwick, Maine, knew when to grab for that brass ring when he was fortunate enough to find this incredible 1966 Sunroof Sedan. Not only is it a low-mileage,

unrestored car, it also came loaded with period accessories installed by the original owner. (That's right, everything on this car was installed when the vehicle was new.)

This amazing find was originally owned by a gentleman named Nathan Tucker. Tucker owned a Volkswagen dealership in Beverly, Massachusetts, and took the pearl white wonder from new car inventory on June 30, 1966,

for his own personal use. Tucker must have liked accessories; as he added a long list of them to personalize his then-new Beetle. He installed Bosch Fanfare horns, bumper guardians, mudflaps, gravel guards, aluminum doorsill trim, Sapphire radio, woodgrain shift knob, parcel tray, underdash tissue box, Coco floor mats, hub cap pullers, trim rings and a Speedwell steering wheel topped off with a sun and moon horn button. Unfortunately, in 1968, Tucker developed health problems, forcing him to sell the dealership. Tucker had his beloved Beetle taken via flatbed truck to his summer home in Gilmanton, New Hampshire. A short time later he passed away, leaving the '66 to his wife. The only drawback was that the Missus has never had a driver's license. After logging just 5,826 miles since new, the Sunroof Sedan was rolled into the garage, the

battery was removed and the car was covered over.

Sometime in 1988 Mrs. Tucker called her grandson over to her house. She thought it might

be a good idea to start up the old Volkswagen; it had not been run since 1968! The grandson purchased a new battery, fired up the '66, and backed it out of the garage. After its first wash in 20 years, the grandson carefully drove the Bug back into the garage, removed the battery and covered the car once more. Over lunch, Mrs. Tucker handed her grandson a large envelope containing all of the original paperwork for the Beetle and gave the car to him. Oddly enough, the grandson had no experience with air-cooled VWs! Incredibly, the car sat otherwise undisturbed until 1995, when Michael got to see it. Michael had first spoken to the grandson in late 1994, and this is when he had first heard about the car. He had been looking for an early Beetle and had just purchased a '54 with 23,500 original miles on the

(continued on page 34)

clock. Michael explained that he would be interested in the '66 as well but it would have to wait until Spring. Winter was closing in and he just did not have the garage space for another vehicle. Michael says that decision haunted him all Winter. Was the '66 improperly stored and completely deteriorated? Or was it a perfectly preserved example?

When Spring arrived, Michael just had to see the car, and so he contacted the grandson. He was amazed to find the vehicle in such excellent condition. The many years of storage had preserved the car almost perfectly. In fact, the only things that needed any attention mechanically were the brakes. And as you can see, the original paint and interior are flawless. A deal was struck, and Michael became the proud new owner of the '66. After bringing his new purchase home, Michael replaced the master cylinder, as well as all four wheel cylinders, using all German parts. He then installed fresh Bosch spark plugs and points, and treated the engine to its first oil change since 1968. All that was left to do was a good detailing. The rest of the car is unrestored. The paint, tires, fan belt, cap and rotor are all the original units from 1966. Michael also received all of the original paperwork from the grandson, including the original sales invoice and window sticker.

Even though this vehicle is very low mileage, Michael does drive it occasionally, and at the time of this writing he has logged a total 6,100 miles on the odometer. The first show this VW attended was the New Hampshire club's VW show in 1997, and it took first in class as well as Best Unrestored honors. Michael reports that to drive this car is like stepping back in time by driving an essentially new car from the '60s. We can see why; this is one of the lowest mileage cars we've ever seen, and definitely the kind of car that most of us can only dream about.

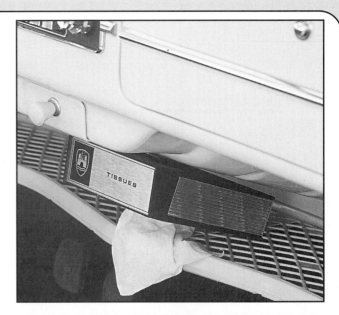

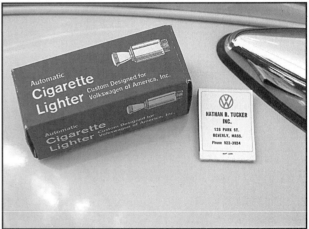

EMERGENCY BRAKE QUICK FIX

8

Text & Photography by Dave Cormack

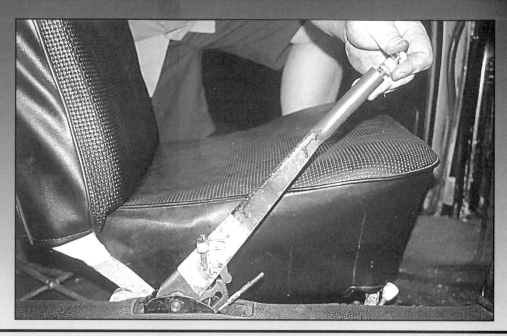

1. This is what happens when you don't adjust your parking (or emergency) brake on time.

You knew it was coming. Every time you pulled up on the emergency brake in your Beetle, the handle kept going higher and higher up. And, rather than take the five or ten minutes it takes to adjust it, you let it slide. The last time you yanked up on the handle, however, the handle came waaaay up, and the button shot out of the handle. Now you can't get it back into the handle where it belongs. C'mon, admit it, this has happened to every one of you at least once. The fix (other than keeping it adjusted properly in the first place), is actually fairly simple.

There is a pawl with teeth on it that is actuated by the rod that just shot out of your parking brake handle. The rod has a crescent shaped bend in it, and this is where the non-tooth end of the pawl is supposed to be. You have to do a little fishing to get everything back into place, but it can be done without dismantling the brake handle. You don't have to remove the seat to effect this cure, but it is a lot easier to get in there with one of the seats out, and this way we can more easily show you how it's done. We will also show you the handle and

pawl assembly out of the car, so you can better see what you will be doing.

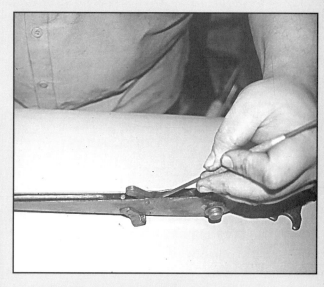

2. The hook on the rod with the button is supposed to fit over the rounded part of the pawl, opposite the part with the teeth on it.

35

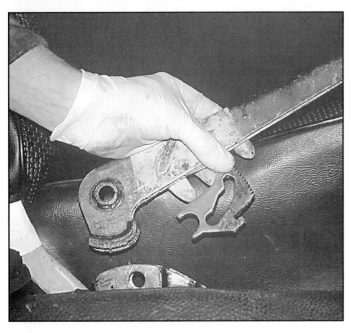

3. We are showing you this out of the car so you can see what it is we are doing. We also removed the piece that fits into the hinge for the handle.

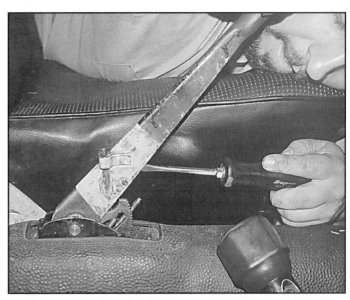

4. With a screwdriver, push the round part of the pawl up into the handle, while pushing on the button, so that the round part of the pawl ends up inside the hook part of the button. To gain enough clearance, you may have to loosen up your parking brake even more or possibly even disconnect the cables.

5. This is what you should have if you are ready to go back together. It's really not that hard, just a little awkward.

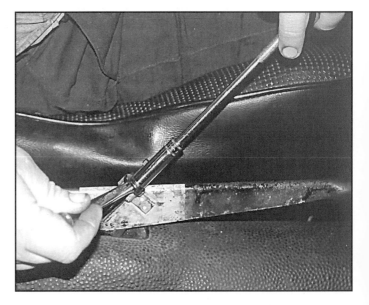

6. Now that you have it back together properly, don't you think it would be a good idea to adjust the cables this time? Loosen up the 10mm lock nut and turn the inside adjusting nut in until you have about 5 to 7 clicks on the handle, from fully released to lock up. Do the same on the other cable. Make sure that when the handle is released you don't have any drag on the rear wheels. If you do, loosen up the adjusting and lock nuts a few turns, equally on each side, until there is no drag on the rear wheels in the released position. This will work on all Beetles from 1956 on up, but you folks with a 1955 and earlier pan will have to adjust your parking brake cables from the front of the car, between the torsion tubes. There is a plate between the torsion tubes that must be removed, and then you will see the cables. They have the same locknut/adjusting nut arrangement that the later cars have, just make sure that you adjust them equally.

MINOR FRONT-END ALIGNMENT

9

Text & Photography by Dave Cormack

Does your Beetle seem to have a mind of its own, drifting all over the road? Does it seem like you're always replacing the front tires? A minor front end alignment may be all your Beetle needs to cure these problems.

Is your Beetle wandering all over the road, and changing lanes on the freeway whenever it feels like it? Are your front tires wearing out at an abnormal rate? With nothing more than a tape measure and a couple of wrenches there may be something you can do at home to remedy this situation. If, at the end of this chapter, you have determined that your king and link pins are worn out, or that your ball joint front beam needs more than just a few simple adjustments, I would suggest that you just save your money and order a rebuilt front beam, as there are tolerances involved that require special tools to set up correctly, and, if you don't know what you are doing, you could end up with a handling problem worse than you already have.

The first thing you want to do is jack up the front of the car so that the wheels are off the ground, and set the car down on some jack stands. Now that the car is secure, grab one of the tires, with one hand at the 6 o'clock position, and the other hand at the 12 o'clock position, and try to wiggle the tire. If you find any play there, refer to Chapter 10 for the how-to on adjusting your front wheel bearings. If the wheel bearing adjustment doesn't take the play out of the front end, you may be facing a front beam rebuild, or a link pin adjustment if your Beetle is a 1964 or earlier. Now grab the wheel and tire at the 9 o'clock and 3 o'clock position, and do the same thing.

You say you have some play? Next thing to try is the steering box adjustment. Take the spare tire out of the car (You do have a properly inflated spare, don't you?) and take off the little inspection cover to the right of the car, as you are looking into the trunk, or, to put it differently, on the side where the steering wheel is. You will see a funny-looking deal with a large (19mm) nut on the side. Loosen this nut up, get a flat-blade screwdriver on the screw that is inside that nut, turn it until you feel it bottom out, then back it out about 1/8 of a turn and tighten down the lock nut. You say you still have some play in the front end? Don't despair, all is still not lost. Crawl back under the car, and take a grease gun with you. Find the little nipples on the torsion bars—there should be four of them—and squirt the grease to them until a little bit comes out of the ends of the torsion tubes. Then, while you are under there, find the link pin carriers. (If your car is a 1964 or earlier you will also find two of those nipples on each side.) Grease them until, once again, you see grease coming out of the knuckle where the spindle turns from the beam. If this doesn't tighten it up you may have some bad tie rods. Check these by having a friend turn the steering wheel while you are under the car. (Now do you see the importance of the jack stands?) If any of the little banjo-looking things attached to the tubes have any side-to-side or up-and-down movement to them they need to be replaced. Some tie rod ends may have grease fittings on them, so give them a squirt of grease also.

As for replacing them, if they show signs of wear, sometimes you get lucky and they will just pop right out, once the cotter key and the retaining nut are removed, but most of the time they require a little force. Resist the temptation to just beat on the threaded part until they pop out. Find a friend with a "pickle fork" that will wedge between the ball joint (or tie rod end) and the arm that attaches to the brake backing plate, and knock it loose that way. This is also the recommended way to get worn ball joints out, too, if you have found any with play in them. I would like to say at this point that nothing will replace a good manual when it comes time to do some serious front-end work.

So we have the wheel bearings adjusted as per specs, and the steering box is adjusted, the tie rod ends have been replaced, along with any worn ball joints; now we need to set the toe-in. The caster (the amount of tilt the spindle has to help the tracking of the car) is set at the factory, and the camber (how much the wheel tilts inward or outward at the top of the wheel), is something that can be adjusted, but not by the average backyard mechanic. Setting the camber requires that the link pin carriers (on the 1964 and earlier cars) be removed and shimmed, which is a little out of reach for the average enthusiast.

1. The first thing we want to do, after making sure the wheel bearings and steering box are properly adjusted, is to grease the torsion assembly, and...

2. & 2a. ...on 1964 and earlier cars, the king and link pin carriers.

If you have a 1964 and earlier link-pin front end, there is one more thing you can do: Adjust the link pins. Right near where you greased the link pin carriers, by the brake backing plate, you will see some cylinder-looking things with clamps on them, and two flat sides that a 14mm wrench will fit onto. There will be one at the top and one at the bottom of the knuckle, two on each side. They may be encrusted with grease, so scrape away until you see what I am talking about. Grab two 17mm wrenches, and a 14mm open end. Remove the cotter keys if the car still has them. Loosen up the clamp with the 17mm open-end wrenches, just enough so you can move the pin with the 14mm open end. Move the pin a few times so you know which way tightens it and which way loosens it. With a pry bar, pry the torsion arm up and down while observing the action of the pin on the carrier. If there is any play, tighten the pin with the 14mm wrench until there is no play at all, and then loosen it just a tiny bit. Then tighten down the clamp. Do this same thing on the other three king and link carriers, top and bottom. It's not as hard as it sounds; once you have done the first one the rest will be easy. Now, do the tire wiggle at 6 o'clock and 12 o'clock routine. If you still have play you either have bad link pins or bad king pins, and you will need a rebuilt front end.

The last thing we can do is set the toe-in, which is how much the front tires point in at the front of the tire. For normal applications, there should be 1/8 inch less distance between the center of the front tires, measured at the front, than in the back. Since you already have the car up on jack stands, go find a tape measure. Measure the distance between the front wheels, from rim edge to rim edge, and write down the measurement; then do the same in the back of the rims. If the measurement is 1/8 of an inch narrower in the front than in the back, then your toe-in is set properly, and you can take your car off the jack stands and take it for a test drive. If there is more or less than the specified 1/8 inch toe-in, you will have to loosen the tie rod ends (those banjo-looking things at the end of the long rods) by prying up the locking tab and loosening the two lock nuts, and turning the tie rods until you have the specified amount of toe-in. Anything more than this is most likely out of the realm of what can be done at home, and, since we are dealing with suspension parts, I believe that it should be turned over to the experts.

(continued on next page)

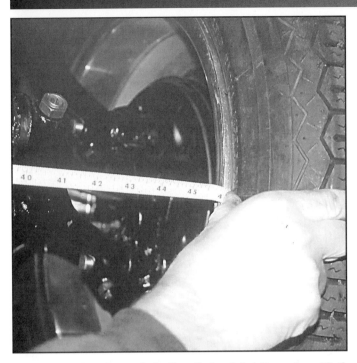

3. & 3a. Setting the toe-in isn't really hard, but it can be a bit time-consuming. Just make sure that the measurement is 1/8-inch narrower in the front than it is in the back.

4. & 4a. Tighten up the king and link pin carriers as outlined in the text.

WHEEL BEARING CONVERSION

10

Text & Photography by Dave Cormack

These are the new bearings, races, grease seals and lock plates from Unique Supply, 610 Tennessee Street, Redlands, CA 92374. (909) 793-0121

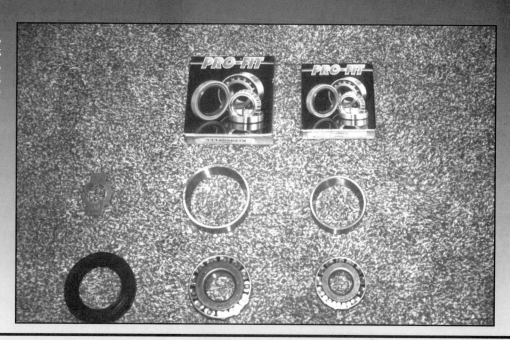

From 1949 to 1965, Volkswagen used ball-type front wheel bearings. In 1966, with the addition of the ball-joint front end, they went to the newer-style tapered roller bearing. Most of the time, the front wheel bearings are not subjected to much abuse. However, in off-road applications, hard cornering or hard braking, these bearings are subjected to tremendous thrust load. Although the early-style bearings are made of very hard metal, their weakness is in the contact area. If you look at an old ball bearing, you can see the amount of area where the ball actually contacts the race is very small. By comparison, the tapered roller bearing has much more of this critical contact area. This means that, in cornering and braking, thrust loads are distributed over a greater area and the bearing will have more resistance to impact damage, such as would be found in an off-road car. Also, in street applications, they are more durable, having more contact area and, when properly adjusted, they don't require replacement as often. So, follow along as we convert these old ball bearings to roller bearings.

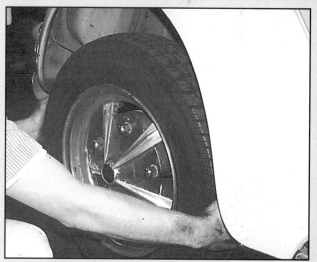

1. Loosen the lug nuts, jack up the car and lower it onto jack-stands. Check bearing play by grabbing the 9 o'clock and 3 o'clock positions of the tire and rock it. If the tie rods are tight and the drum moves but not the brake backing plate, chances are the wheel bearings are worn and need adjustment or replacement. Remove the cotter pin from the center of the dust cover and push the speedometer cable through the dust cover.

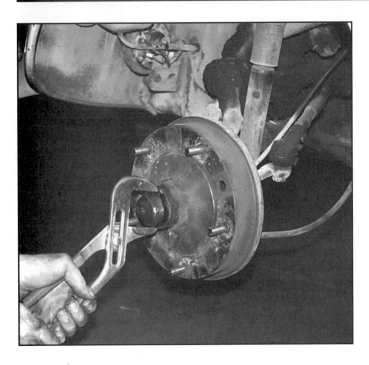

2. Use a pair of channel lock-type pliers to pry off the dust cover. You may also tap the cover with a hammer while rotating the drum and cover to knock the cover off.

3. Bend the locking tab away from the front spindle lock nut.

4. & 4a. Unscrew the outer nut. If you have any drag on the brake drum from the shoes, now is the time to adjust down your brakes so the drum will come off easily. Now unscrew the inner nut and pull off the brake drum.

5. & 5a. Carefully separate the inner bearing race from the spindle with a chisel. Be very gentle so as not to damage the spindle. Once you have moved it a little, you can use a crow's foot or other suitable tool to pry it off the rest of the way.

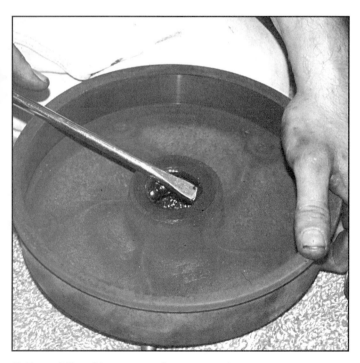

6. Pry out the old grease seal.

7. Using a long drift punch, knock out the outer bearing race.

8. Turn the drum over and knock out the inner bearing race. Take the inner bearing out, clean the drum with solvent and let it dry.

9. Using a hammer, start the new inner race in the drum. Knock it all the way in, ensuring that the wider end is toward the outside of the drum.

10. & 10a. This is what the inner race looks like when it is all the way in.

11. Now do the same with the outer race. Using a long drift punch, tap gently until it is all the way in, as shown above.

12. Pack the inner and outer wheel bearing with bearing grease. We cheated and used a pressure-type greaser, but the old "hand-packing" method works just as well—it's just messier.

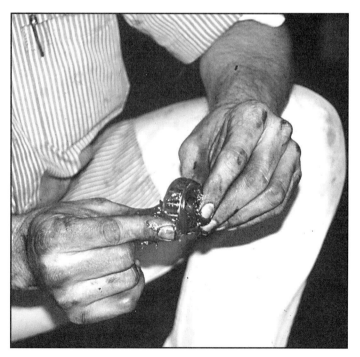

13. Work the grease into all of the rollers, and into the recess between the rollers and the outer cage.

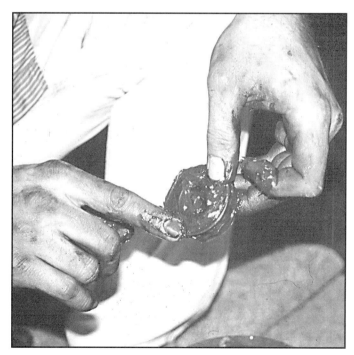

14. Apply a light coat of grease to the inner and outer races.

15. Set the inner bearing in its race, and place the grease seal in the drum. Pound down the grease seal with a hammer, moving around the seal, until it is flush with the drum. Install the drum back onto the spindle.

16. Place the outer bearing in the race, and reinstall the thrust washer.

17. Thread the inner adjusting nut onto the spindle. Make sure the brake shoes do not touch the drum, then tighten the adjusting nut to about 11 ft-lbs to seat the bearings and align the rollers against the race. Now, back the adjusting nut off until there is 0.0012 to 0.0048 inches of end play. Don't rock or shake the durm, just give it an even pull inward and outward. If you don't have access to a dial indicator, you can tighten the nut until you can just barely move the thrust washer with a screwdriver as shown at left. Now, back the adjusting nut out just a little bit so the washer moves a tiny bit more freely. *It is very important that you do not overtighten the bearings!* This should provide just a slight rocking when the durm is rocked from side to side.

18. Place the new locking tab over the the inner adjusting nut, and thread the outer locking nut onto the spindle. Making sure you don't disturb the inner nut, tighten down the lock nut. An open-end wrench with the flat part filed or ground down comes in handy; these nuts are pretty thin.

19. Bend the lock tab down around the flat side of both nuts, one tab for each nut.

20. Apply a thin coat of grease to the dust cover where it goes into the drum, push the speedometer cable through the square hole in the cover and knock the dust cover into the drum. Install the cotter pin in the end of the speedometer cable, readjust your brakes, put your wheels back on and lower the car to the ground.

11

A CLASSIC '62

by Karl Funke. Photography by Henry Z. DeKuyper

Scott Breeden still remembers going with his dad to the Oceanside, Calif.-based Don Sharp VW dealership to pick up their brand new Volkswagen Beetle in 1962. One thing he clearly recalls is playing with the windshield squirter while the car was still in the showroom (the squirter actually worked back then). These memories are so etched into his brain, Scott decided to experi-

ence seeing the car "for the first time" again. So, 36 years later, after the old Bug's odometer had already turned over three times and the sheetmetal had been banged up a bit, Scott took it in to West Coast Classic Restoration in Fullerton, Calif., to have the old beater freshened up. Lenny Copp, the shop's proprietor, decided it was a perfect candidate for a full restoration, but warned Scott that carrying this

work out would not be cheap; it would, in fact, cost more than the car was actually worth. However, as usually happens with a project like this, love of the car won out and Scott really had no choice but to go the full resto route.

At first, the project was only going to be a body and drivetrain restoration (but we all know how that goes). The car was disassembled and sent off to the body shop where Tony Ochoa and the WCC crew started work on it. Then one day Scott came by for a visit and just happened to spot, up on one of the shop's lifts, a complete chassis which had been detailed and powdercoated in preparation for a show. "Wow!" he exclaimed, indicating the detailed chassis. "What if I want that? How much more?" After a little bit of coercion Scott was able to convince Lenny to perform a full powdercoating job on his Bug. The entire chassis was stripped in preparation—when powdercoating, everything and anything that can be taken off must be removed—and the individual pieces were sent off to be coated, including the chassis itself, rear spring plates, all backing plates and the front torsion arms.

Tony Ochoa was responsible for straightening out the body panels and respraying the Bug in its original Ivory color (paint code L87). While he was doing this, Phillip Diaz went to work reassembling the newly powdered chassis, and Rafael installed all new rubber bushings, moldings, etc., on the body. Rafael also installed the new wire harness, pulling it through the car without ever once looking at a wiring diagram—he's that good. Everything which needed replacing during the restoration process was exchanged with a genuine German part, including all chassis pieces, brake hoses, wheel cylinders and cables; hard-to-find parts were sourced from Wolfsburg West and BFY Obsolete Parts in Anaheim and Orange, Calif., respectively.

The wheels were also subjected to a little preferential treatment in order to restore them to their original finish. The first time around they were powdercoated all black, then just the fronts were refinished in ivory, and the inside rims were coated with tan. Lenny said this is the way the factory finished the wheels when the car was built in 1962. While all this was happening, Jessie Quintana was preparing the new headliner and fitting the seat covers to the front and rear seats. The car originally came with heat-pleated seat covers, accordingly TMI seat covers were settled on for originality sake and matching TMI door panels were installed as well. The interior carpet was replaced with original German square weave, and the new floor mats were obtained from Wolfsburg West.

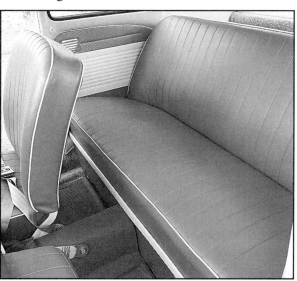

Lenny's friends Boozer and Kevin of Elite Foreign Auto in Fullerton rebuilt the engine with fully powdercoated tin and shiny new hardware to fit with the car's new look. No performance mods were carried out; the powerplant remains a stock 40 horse. The original transmission was taken to Rancho Performance Transaxles in Anaheim where it was rebuilt to stock specifications right down to the one-piece axle boots and left unpainted for originality sake.

(continued on page 52)

After all the individual parts were finished separately they were consolidated in the West Coast Classics shop and reassembly was begun. Lenny said this is everyone's favorite part of the restoration process: Seeing the car in a 100 pieces, then putting it back together and driving it soon thereafter. When it was finally together again, the first trip this Bug made was to Community Tire in Brea, Calif., for a four-wheel alignment; Lenny said he hated the drive there but loved the drive back, attesting to the great difference an alignment can make on ride quality. When Scott finally came to get his car, the West Coast Classics staff was sad to see their baby go, but at the same time delighted to have been part of the restoration and to have done such a great job on Mr. Breeden's "new" first love.

WEBER IDA CARB CONVERSION KIT

12

Text & Photography by Dave Cormack

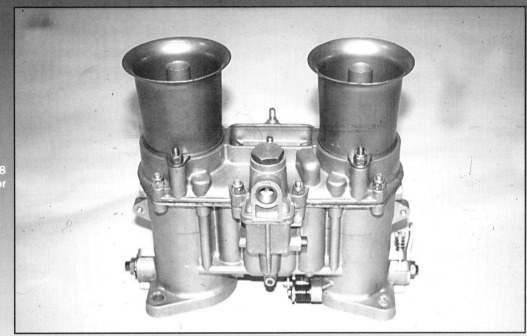

1. Here is a stock 48 IDA carburetor, ready for the Sacchette touch.

If you have ever seen a P.R.A. (Professional Racer's Association) event, you have no doubt heard of Jack Sacchette. He is one of the best-known names in the Pro Stock category, and won the Pro Stock championship in 1989, 1990, 1991 and 1997. This guy absolutely lives and breathes VW high performance. He has been responsible for many innovations in the VW drag racing industry, one for which is this conversion for the 48 IDA Weber carburetor. Jack recognized the need to increase flow capacities of the stock carb, and since no one else was doing it at the time, he did it himself.

Jack offers this conversion either as a do-it-yourself kit with complete and detailed instructions, or you can send him your carbs and he will perform the work at his shop, Jaycee Enterprises in Huntington Beach, California. He also has some neat tricks he learned from his years of racing the 48 IDA that can be used on all-out race machines or on street machines. Jack has a

dyno facility, flow bench, engine building service, and just about anything else you can think of pertaining to making a VW go fast. We watched as Jack disassembled, bored and modified the float bowl, and installed a set of his Pro Stock velocity stacks on a stock 48 IDA carb. Since this carb would be used on the street, Jack added another progression circuit in the throttle bore that allows the carb to idle and run through the powerband smoothly. Also on the list were a float bowl conversion and a set of Pro Stack Velocity stacks.

SOURCE
Jaycee Enterprises
7442 Talbert Ave.
Huntington Beach, CA 92647
714/848-9898
www.jaycee-ent.com

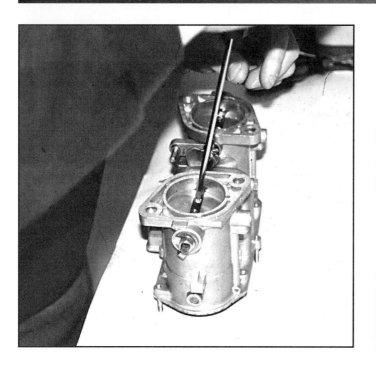

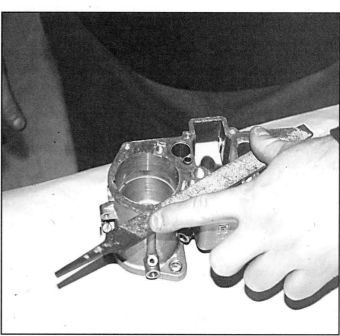

2. The butterfly screws are removed and discarded. In addition, the studs that hold the top of the carb are replaced with Allen bolts provided in the kit. Also, the pin holding the linkage arm and spring is driven out with a small drift punch.

3. The flat part of the main body is checked by running a file over the top. This removes any imperfections that would interfere with the seal between the two halves of the carb.

4. A special chuck was made for his lathe to hold the carburetor. Here we see the carb held in place, ready for the machining process.

5. Several passes are made on the lathe, removing a tiny bit of material each time until the required measurement is achieved.

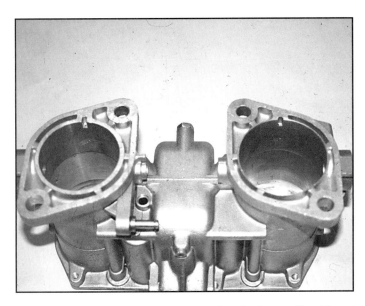

6. On the left is the stock bore, on the right is the machined bore. Note how much material is removed.

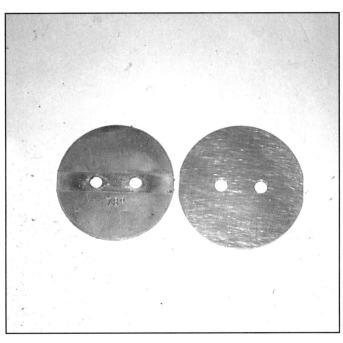

7. Another example of the difference can be seen in the different sizes of the butterflies. The stock unit is on the left, the Jaycee 51.5mm unit on the right.

8. & 8a. Since this carb was going to receive the "full treatment," Jack machined the top of the carb (left photo) for some of his Pro Stock velocity stacks. The stack on the left in the right photo is the Jaycee Pro Stock unit.

10. Since this carb will be used on the street, Jack added another progression circuit at the 1 o'clock position, which allows a smoother transition from idle to low and midrange.

9. In addition to milling the top of the carb for velocity stacks, Jack also drills and taps the hole where the plug was; this is where a set screw need to be installed to hold th auxilliary venturi in place. Normally, the venturi is held in place by the velocity stack, but with the Jaycee Pro Stock units, this is no longer possible because the venturis will move up and down in the throttle bores without this modification. The venturi is now held in place by a 7/16-20 set screw, which is included in the velocity stack conversion kit.

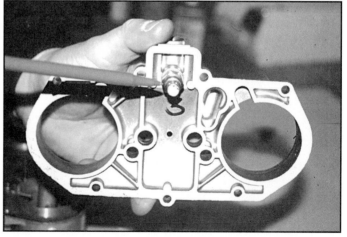

11. In an effort to keep from running out of fuel on the top end of the drag strip, the float bowls are modified by machining out the wall between the float bowl and this cavity, which was nothing but unused space.

12. & 12a. Along with this float bowl mod, Jack also drills out the fuel inlet in the top of the carb body (top photo) and installs one of his own glass ball needle valves (bottom photo).

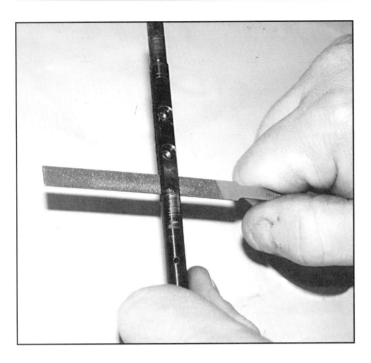

13. With the machining of the carb body finished, a slot is opened up in the throttle shaft for larger butterflies.

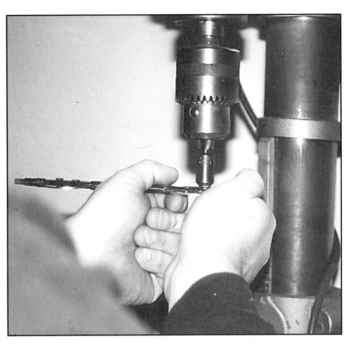

14. Holes are countersunk in the throttle shaft for the new Allen screws (provided in the conversion kit).

15. After the butterflies are assembled on the shaft with the new Allen screws, the protruding portions of the threads are milled off.

16. Now everything is thoroughly washed and then dried with compressed air, ensuring all the air and fuel passages are open.

17. These are all of the components, ready for assembly.

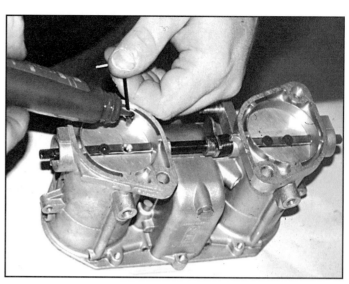

18. The assembly process is started by taking the butterflies out of the throttle shafts, using care to ensure the Allen screws stay with their respective holes in the throttle shaft. While making sure the butterflies are aligned in their respective bores, Jack installs the Allen screws, one at a time, using a dab of Loctite®.

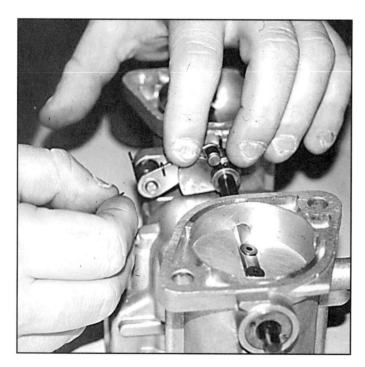

19. With the butterflies installed, moving freely, and seating against the bores properly, the accelerator lever and return spring are installed and the locking pin put back.

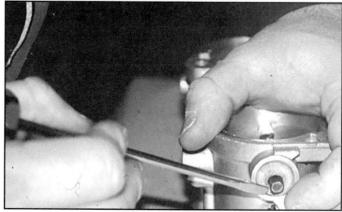

20. & 20a. Next, the throttle shaft bearings are greased and installed, (top) followed by the dust covers (bottom).

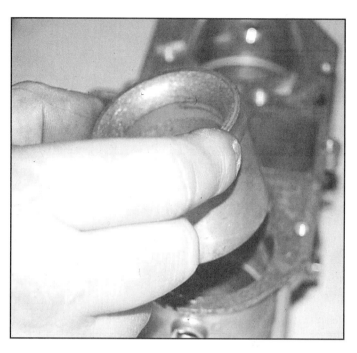

21. Now comes the accelerator pump lever and spring. After the new glass ball needle valve is installed, the float is put back into place. The glass ball needle valve will eliminate flooding caused by the heavier steel ball, allowing for more fuel pressure. Jack says up to 9 pounds of fuel pressure can be used when this needle valve is installed.

22. The venturis are next on the installation list; these are the 37mm units that came with the carb. Jaycee manufactures and sells venturis ranging in size from 40mm to 48mm.

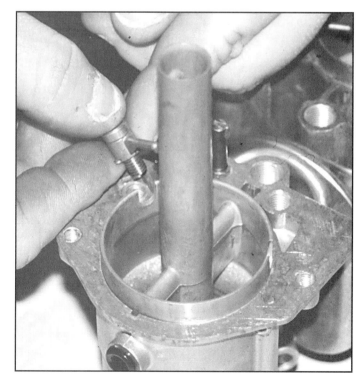

23. The auxilliary venturis are next, held in place by the Jaycee set screw. Afterward, the accelerator pump squirters are installed.

24. The progression plugs are next.

25. Jack puts Blue Dykem, or uses a felt pen, to paint the bottom of the jet stack to ensure the stack is seating properly.

26. The top of the carb is put on with the new Allen bolts supplied in the kit.

27. The Jaycee Pro Stock velocity stacks are next. These were computer designed using CAD to provide maximum air speed and velocity. They come anodized in either red, blue or plain finishes.

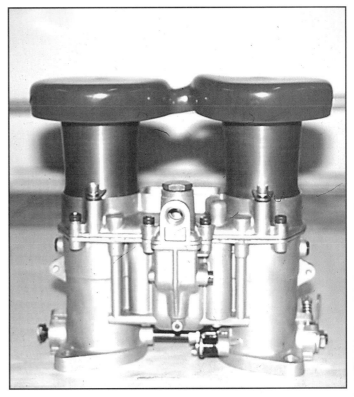

28. Here is the finished product, ready to install, with new dust covers to fit the new stacks. Another nice feature is that if you later want to jump up to the Jaycee 62mm Terminator carbs, Jack will take your 48 or 51.5mm carbs in trade on Terminators.

ENGINE REMOVAL

13

Text & Photography by D.E. Meyer

1. Raise the vehicle and position it on the jackstands. First place a 4x4 in front of each front wheel to keep the car from rolling down the driveway while you're jacking it up. Jack up one side at a time using the floor jack, positioning it at the stock VW jack point. Then position a jackstand under the torsion housing. You don't need to have the car really high at this point, we're just getting it high enough to make working underneath it easier. Just get the rear tires off the ground about two inches or so. Now, go to the other side of the car and do the same thing.

There are many repairs or problems that will require removing the engine from your VW. For example, driving around without the fan belt can result in complete engine meltdown and a rebuild. But you will also need to remove the engine to replace a bad clutch or to fix major oil leaks, or just to replace it.

Get Prepared

To complete this task, you'll need to plan and prepare ahead of time. There is a general procedure to removing a VW engine that can be applied to many models.

A Clean Car—If the car runs, drive it to a car wash with an engine degreaser and thoroughly spray wash the engine compartment and underneath the car. Pay particular attention to the area between the engine and transmission where it gets the dirtiest. The better you do the job, the happier you'll be later when lying under the car.

Workspace—Of course, a nice garage would be best, but any cement floor will do. You could do all this in the dirt if you absolutely had to, but I wouldn't recommend it. For one thing it's just too easy to lose little parts. Also, the ground may not provide enough stability for a jackstands and a floorjack. Besides, who wants to work in the dirt?

Floorjack and Jackstands—Don't try to use the little bottle-jack from your wife's Honda. Buy, borrow or rent a good floor jack and at least two good jackstands

for support. The floorjack is critical not just for lifting the car, but also for removing the engine.

Wood—Find a couple 4x4s and 2x4s, 12 to 16 inches long and a 1x6 about 12 inches long. You'll use the 1x6 between the jack and the engine and you'll use two of the 4x4s to block the tires to keep the car from rolling away while you try to work on it. The others will be put between the jack and the car in a couple of places.

Rags and Hand Cleaner—Good shop rags, and plenty of them, along with a good automotive-quality hand cleaner are recommended.

Tools—If you don't have at least a small toolbox with an assortment of metric wrenches, some screwdrivers, a pair of pliers, and an adjustable-end wrench, then you shouldn't undertake the task. More likely, you wouldn't be considering the job in the first place. So make sure you have the correct assortment of tools.

Paper Cups—Several small cups or coffee cans are a good idea for holding all the little bolts, nuts and miscellaneous fasteners. Have something to label the cups if necessary.

Pencil and Paper—You'll need a pen or pencil for making notes and listing any needed new part. Get a notebook for the job. Also, you'll need a pencil for plugging the fuel line when you disconnect it.

Masking Tape—Use this to mark wires as they are disconnected so you'll remember where they go during reinstallation.

2. Open the engine compartment lid and remove the air cleaner. Be careful: if it's the stock air cleaner it is filled with oil. Once you pull it off, and before you proceed any further, it would be a good time to clean the air filter. Once this is done and new oil is added, set it aside. Cover the top of the carburetor to prevent dirt or small parts from falling in—either a rag or masking tape works.

3. Disconnect the battery cable before going any further. The battery in stock Volkswagens is located under the back seat on the passenger's side. Lift up the seat bottom, loosen the bolt on the ground strap and remove it. Check to see if the battery posts are clean. With paper and pencil, begin your parts list with new battery post pads. Check the cables and clamps for signs of corrosion. If they have any, or are worn, they should be replaced now. Next begin disconnecting all other electrical wires connected to the engine. One wire connects to the coil and one connects to the choke actuator. The rest are connected to the generator, alternator and voltage regulator, depending on the year and model of your VW.

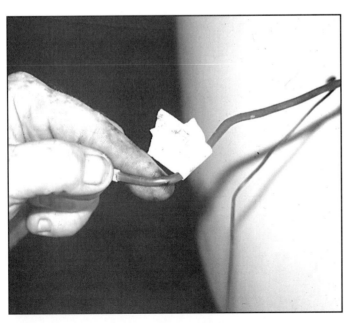

4. As you remove the wires, the best thing you can do is to wrap a small piece of tape around each wire, then label the wire indicating where it goes. Then tape the wires to the fender so they are out of the way. Disconnect the accelerator cable and push the end of the cable back through the opening in the shroud. Now, reach around to the back of the engine and pull the cable through the rest of the way.

5. Remove the rear engine compartment tin. Use a big, flat screwdriver and remove the rear engine tin screws. If you have a newer car with fresh air heater hoses, then you will have to remove them first; they should just pull off. If they are in bad shape—and they usually are—then put a new set on your parts list. Next, remove the small tin shroud around the crankshaft pulley and the two even smaller ones around the manifold heat risers. Then remove the main piece of the rear shroud. It will just lift up and out.

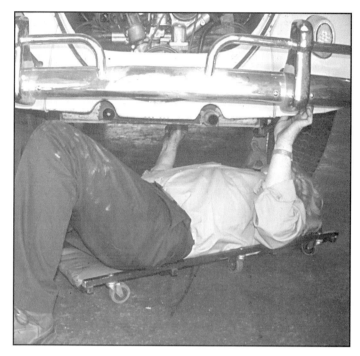

6. Remove the upper engine bolts/nuts. These are large 17mm bolts that connect the engine to the transmission. On the passenger side, one of these bolts also serves as one of the starter mounts. They are next to impossible to see as they are located behind the engine and out of sight. You probably will need to use either a box-end or open-end wrench to get to them. Be patient, get as comfortable as you can, reach back there and be prepared to turn them little by little.

7. Before going any further, check to make sure the jackstands are still secure. This is a good thing to do throughout the process. Tugging and pushing on bolts may cause you to shift the car enough so the jackstands are no longer secure. Better to be safe than dead. Disconnect the bellows from the heater boxes. Use a trouble light so you can see what you're doing. The heater box bellows are the large, stiff, rubber flex hoses from the exhaust system to a round metal duct that runs up to the body. They should just slip off.

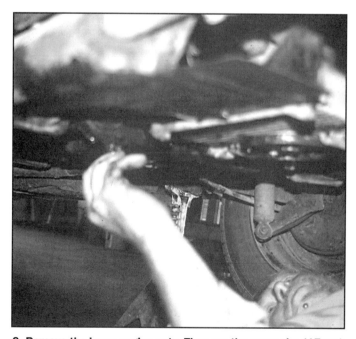

8. Disconnect the heater control cables. Use a 10mm wrench and perhaps the pliers to hold the attachment still while you unscrew them. Disconnect the fuel line and clamp it off or stuff the old pencil into the end of the line. Be careful to do this from a distance; gasoline in the eyes or ears is no fun.

9. Remove the lower engine nuts. They are the same size (17mm) as the upper bolts. Don't worry as you remove them, the engine will not fall out on top of you; it will still be held in by the studs they are threaded on, along with the output shaft. Once these are removed, take a breather and look around a little. Did you forget anything? Is everything out of the way?

10. Place the 1x6 piece of wood on top of the floorjack, then place the jack under the engine so the wood and the jack will center on the oil drain plate. Slowly raise the jack just about an inch, maybe less. You want to raise the engine just enough so it does not land on the studs or input shaft. Put one hand on top of the fan shroud and the other on the muffler. Now, slowly pull the jack and the engine back toward you. This will pull the studs through the lower tranny mounts and the output shaft out of the transmission shaft hole.

11. Slowly lower the jack and the engine to the ground. Keep an eye on the studs and the output shaft to make sure they don't hang up on anything as you lower the engine. You need to do all this very slowly, so watch out for any possible hang-ups.

12. Now raise the car higher. If you are lucky enough to have two floorjacks, continue. If you have only one, you'll want to retrieve it. Lay one of the 2x4s on the floor underneath the exhaust system heater box. Stick another one under the other side. Pry one side of the exhaust up and pull the jack out. Roll the floorjack under the car with a couple of 4x4s on top. Place the center of the jack under the main frame horns of the pan. This is the spot where the center tunnel divides into two smaller tubes to go around the transmission and engine.

13. Now, jack the car up high enough to slide the engine out from under the rear bumper. Slide the engine out. Don't forget to lower the car back down onto the jackstands.

VINTAGE ENGINE REBUILD, PART I

14

Text & Photography by Hank Roed

1. A 1954 36 hp engine complete with rusted out single tip muffler and unknown mileage awaits surgery on the engine stand.

From 1954 through 1960, the Volkswagen Bug came from the factory with a 64mm stroke by 77mm bore 1192cc 36 hp engine by S.A.E. testing. In European rating it was 36 hp D.I.N.

Compared to most cars on the road of that era it was, well, a real wimp, but that's the way Volkswagen intended it. They knew the simplest, most inexpensive way to get long engine life to match the sturdy chassis and body was to deliberately restrict the performance of the engine. In design, this was attained by restricted breathing. It has a very small diameter carb venturi and intake manifold matched to small valves with low lift and cam timing more suited to a tractor. When this strangled breathing system is combined with a 6.6:1 compression ratio and top gear ratio of 3.52:1, you end up with a piston speed of only 1400 feet per minute when the car is flat out. Full throttle, pedal to the metal flat out is how you drove these cars on the highways. No, it doesn't hurt a bit. The predominant misunder-

standing was to drive them too slow. Lugging the engine was the killer. Many drivers of this era had just traded in their long stroke six- or eight-cylinder car and tried driving downhill at the speed limit and then all the way uphill in fourth gear. The more informed drivers drove downhill as fast as possible to gain momentum for the oncoming uphill, and when the rpm dropped, began rowing down through the gears in an attempt to keep the engine near its peak powerband of about 3700 rpm.

I have even heard of some daring drivers jury-rigging a suicide cruise control on cross-country trips, a stick wedged between the seat and gas pedal. Yes, they arrived safely with no harm to the engine or any speeding tickets and averaged about 30 mpg.

To restore a 1954 through 1960 Volkswagen to original condition requires the rebuilding of a 36 hp engine, preferably with the original engine cases or at least a

(continued on next page)

serial number in series with your chassis number.

Hopefully, this article will enable the novice to build his first engine, but even if you have experience with the later engines, it may be helpful to note some of the differences in design. You won't need a Snap-On toolbox the size of a refrigerator. Basic metric wrenches and sockets, etc. will do for the most part with the exception of a few special tools that you can either borrow, or have a Volkswagen shop do for you. Machining of course will necessitate a machine shop.

If your car is missing the engine they are relatively inexpensive as a core from salvage yards, swap meets, VW club members. The main visual identification other than the serial numbers is a one-piece generator stand, which is an integral part of the right engine case and horizontal fuel pump on the left side. Try to get one that hasn't been stored outdoors and turns over by hand.

Check the endplay by pushing and pulling on either the lower pulley or the flywheel. Clunk is not good; 0.005" is good. Being able to hear it run is even better. Factory wear limit on a compression test 60 lbs/sq-in; 100-114 lbs/sq-in is the normal reading of a new

engine. When new, oil pressure (with SAE 20 oil) is 7 lbs/sq-in at idle speed when warmed up. At 2500 rpm it is 28 lbs/sq-in.

Try to get an engine as complete as possible. Most heater boxes and mufflers will be rusted out. Mufflers are available but heater boxes are more difficult to find in good condition.

If possible, steam-clean it before disassembly and your shop, barn, kitchen table or hotel room will stay a lot cleaner. A VW engine stand is the preferred way to go and is available as a simple bench mount or a roll-around model. A repair manual is helpful. These have been published by Bentley, Haynes and others but be sure it is for a 36 hp engine. In this chapter, we used the VW factory manual for most specifications plus a few tips learned from experience. Most parts needed are available from various companies specializing in vintage VWs.

When prepping the sheet metal, it is recommended to bead-blast or chemically strip the old paint. You can have it painted by an automotive painter, powder coated, or do it yourself with spray cans of Krylon® which

2. Drain the oil using a 10mm socket and remove the plate and screen. Some of the studs may stick to the nuts and come out of the case. Don't worry, we will tend to that later. A touch of your finger can indicate internal damage. Look for anything metallic or use a magnet. Worn bearings may show up as gray oil. Spray all the nuts and bolts with penetrating oil and then remove the heat riser bolts with a 10mm socket. They will often snap off in the muffler due to rust and heat. If re-using the muffler you will need to drill and re-tap the threads. Here it isn't a problem, as a new single tip muffler will be going back on. Remove the sheet metal screws on the heater channels, and with a 13mm or 14mm socket, remove the nuts mating the muffler to the cylinder heads. 14mm is the original size on 36 hp engines.

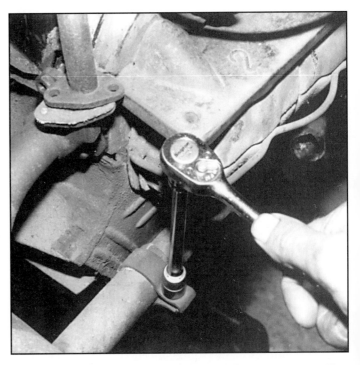

3. Loosen the clamps that secure the header pipes to the muffler. On 36 hp engines this is a straight slip fit without gaskets or asbestos donuts as on later engines. Remove all remaining sheet metal screws. To save time disassembling, whatever tool you have in your hand try to use it on everything it fits.

seems to work best. The black sheet metal was originally a semi-gloss or semi-flat type. The gray on the heater junction boxes and intake manifold was again semi-flat or semi-gloss, but heat resistant. The generator strap and coil bracket were plated and not painted, so they could just be sanded or polished, then sprayed with Krylon clear spray. The clear spray could also be used on polished fuel lines, vacuum lines,the generator nut etc.

To save you grief, one area of difficulty I encountered was locating the correct size main bearings. They come in various sizes such as oversize O.D. for a line bore case and undersized I.D.—0.010" or 0.025mm. Some also have an oversize thrust surface on the rear main for a case re-machined at the thrust. They are no longer in production and many of the most commonly used sizes are difficult to locate. Consequently, it is advisable after disassembly and before line boring your case or regrinding the crank to locate the needed bearings; you may even need a different crank or case to come up with the correct combination.

Another hard-to-find item seems to be the shims for adjusting the flywheel end play. This is part of the treasure hunting aspect of vintage restoration, which some people hate, and others enjoy immensely when they finally find what they have been hunting for. On the plus side, all the vintage cars restored to original condition continue to appreciate along with pride of ownership. As an investment, would you rather invite friends over to see your car or your stock portfolio?

Volkswagens achieved cult status right from the beginning, with drivers waving at each other in recognition and bumper stickers proclaiming, "You have just been passed by 36 hp." Some were happy to see the later models arrive with more horsepower and either traded in their cars or discovered it was an easy engine swap.

Worldwide, the original 36 hp engines carried many people all over the world throughout their lives and also served as cheap, lightweight, reliable mobile transportation for many fixed or mobile industrial applications.

4. Remove the front sheet metal that seals at the firewall. Note the grommet on the fuel lines. When this is worn or missing the sheet metal will cut into the fuel line. You may need to replace both.

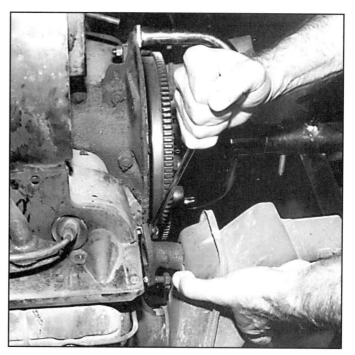

5. Remove the heater channel assemblies as a complete unit. Shown here is the right side for number 1 and 2 cylinders as stamped on the cylinder head covers.

6. Loosen the thermostat under number 1 and 2 cylinders first and then unbolt the bracket from the case. Unscrew the copper thermostat bellows from a rod between the cylinders.

7. Wedge a screwdriver in a slot on the generator pulley against a bolt head in the generator, remove the generator pulley nut. Note the shims used between the two pulley halves. These are used to adjust the fan belt tension by increasing or decreasing the pinch on the wedge shape of the fan belt. The remaining shims are stored under the pulley nut. You must have a total of enough shims that the nut will tighten on the shims and not bottom out the generator shaft threads.

8. Loosen the generator strap and slide it towards the fan shroud. With the fan belt, coil wire, all sheet metal screws and throttle cable guide removed, lift off the fan shroud with fan and generator as a unit. With a 10mm socket, remove the four screws holding the generator backing plate to the fan shroud.

9. Remove the two fuel lines and metal vacuum advance line, which runs from the distributor to the right rear of the carburetor.

10. If you took my advice to use the one tool whenever possible, you will have already removed the four nuts that clamp the intake manifold to the cylinder head, and you can just lift off the intake manifold.

11. Remove the cylinder covers from both sides. Remove the two nuts beneath the oil cooler and one in the top with a 10mm wrench. Try not to lose the hardware. It will be needed later.

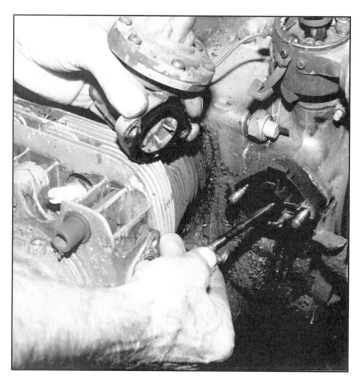

12. Remove the fuel pump with a 14mm socket and extension. Next the fuel pump rod and note the end towards the engine is different in that it has beveled edges. Remove the fuel pump spacer block and check for cracks, usually caused by over tightening in an attempt to fix leaks.

13. Unbolt the distributor clamp from the block and lift it out. Remove the oil pressure-warning switch.

14. If you rotate the valve cover off like this you can prevent oil spillage. Note the gasket stuck to the head. Never use adhesive next to the head, only towards the valve cover.

15. To pry off the lower pulley without a puller tool, use the pry bars a wiggle it off. Pry against the two screws behind the pulley and not against the soft engine case.

16. Remove the two screws behind the pulley and the piece of sheet metal.

17. Unbolt the rocker arm shaft. Note the rocker shafts mount differently than later engines in that the casting in the head is a half circle and a curved metal cap is on top.

18. When you remove the pushrods you will notice that the cam followers are an integral part of the pushrod, unlike later model engines. The radius on the followers should be checked for wear and make sure the oil passages are clear. If the pushrods were ever soaked in carburetor cleaner they may be plugged. This may or may not be because they were designed with a wood insert inside to absorb noise. Whatever the reason, if this would swell up, the oil flow would be restricted or stopped.

19. Prior to 1956, the cylinder head nuts were the same as used on Porsche and require a 10mm hex wrench or Allen wrench. From 1956 on, hex head nuts are used on the flat part of the head. Loosen all cylinder head nuts alternately, taking care not to lock the cylinder head. If a nut is frozen to the stud, use channel-lock pliers to prevent the stud from coming out of the case. It can be removed, but every time it is, it will fit a bit looser.

20. Gently pry the cylinder head loose but not completely off. Here, I use a magnet to retrieve all the cylinder head washers. Six of them have a larger O.D. than the later engines. The two in the recessed holes are smaller I.D.

21. Remove the cylinder heads. This one comes off with the pushrod tubes and seal stuck in place.

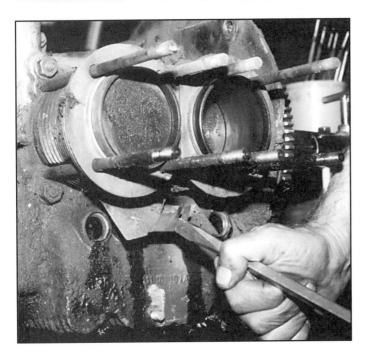

22. Remove the air deflector plates. They are very important as they deflect the air blown down from the fan to flow around the cylinders for more even cooling.

23. If the air deflector plates fit poorly, you may want to drill two holes and wire them to the top cylinder studs.

24. Removing the cylinder may require some prying. Pry away from the case taking care not to gouge the cylinder seating surface of the case. Prying must be done evenly to prevent locking the cylinder in the case bore. While prying from the top use a soft mallet to tap on the bottom. This will usually wiggle the cylinder off.

25. You will need some sort of wrist pin driver to tap them out of the pistons. This one is an old cylinder head stud with two old barrel nuts. One nut is run all the way up on the threads, leaving a portion to fit inside the wrist pin. Hold the piston while tapping with a hammer to prevent bending the connecting rod.

26. Place the engine short block on the bench. Install a flywheel lock and remove the pressure plate bolts alternating the removal sequence.

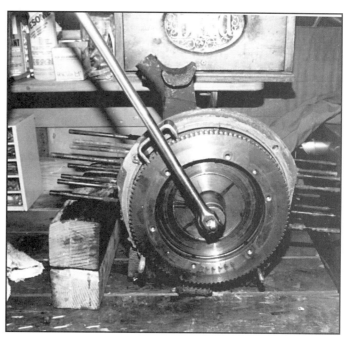

27. Where there's a will, there's a way. Brace the engine, using a long breaker bar or air impact gun, then remove the gland nut with a 36mm socket.

28. Unlike the later engines, the 36 hp has two bolts pinching the cam plug and must be removed with a 10mm wrench before any attempt is made to separate the case halves.

29. Pry out the flywheel seal, or rear main seal. Do not gouge the case. Note the depth in the case; it is flush as opposed to the later models, which are recessed. Behind the seal are the three shims used to adjust the crankshaft end play. They are smaller in diameter than later model engines. They are made in varying thickness but are hard to find.

30. With the engine back on the stand, remove the four oil pump cover nuts with a 10mm socket. Around the perimeter of the case are two different size nuts. Use a 10mm and 14mm socket to remove. Remove the six main nuts and washers near the cylinder bores with a 17mm socket.

31. While lifting up on the generator stand, tap the case studs with a mallet enough to loosen the case halves.

32. After the case halves are loosened, the oil pump can be removed. Slight coaxing may be needed; if so, pry away from the case. A gouge here would surely leak oil.

33. While wiggling the case half and tapping on the case studs with a mallet the case half will loosen and lift straight off; do not pry between the case halves.

34. Remove the camshaft. The early gear on the cam was a soft fiber. Most have been upgraded to aluminum gears, as they were prone to wear.

35. Grasp the crank by the number 1 and 2 connecting rods, and lift it out of the case.

36. Remove the split center main bearing and cam plug. Also remove the other half of the bearing from the other case half. Remove the four main bearing dowel pins from the left case half and one dowel pin from the right case half.

37. Remove the distributor drive gear and thrust washer. There may be two washers but keep them with the drive gear so as not to confuse them with other similar washers from the engine.

38. With a square shank screwdriver and crescent wrench, remove the oil pressure relief valve plug. The plug is hollow with a spring inside. Using a magnet, screwdriver or folded piece of wire, remove the oil pressure relief valve from the case.

39. An easy to make crank holder is a gland nut welded to a piece of metal and clamped in a vise. Using a drift punch, drive out the Woodruff key, then pry and remove the slinger ring and bearing.

40. Remove the snap ring with special snap ring pliers.

41. A Gene Berg gear puller and a screwdriver are used with a rag to keep the crank from turning as the gears are pulled off. Another method is to clamp a two-piece plate under the gear and press the crank off the gear with a hydraulic press, but the Berg gear puller is the way to go.

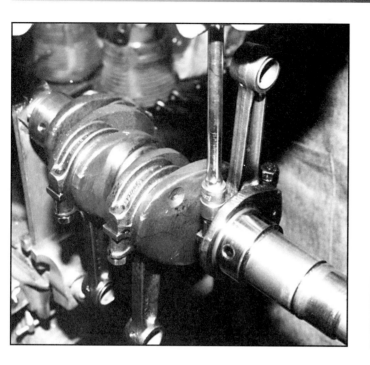

42. As you remove the rods, keep the bolts and caps together. The rods and caps have matching numbers.

43. Note how the thumb and forefinger are holding the bolts in place as they are removed. There was very little left of this burned rod bearing.

44. The rod journal also shows excessive abuse and lack of oil; this crankshaft will have to be reground or replaced.

45. A micrometer is not needed to check the rod journal at this point, as the metric numbers on the rod bearing, 050, indicate it is the second undersized or 0.020". To regrind the crank would require going to 075 or 0.030". You should not use a crank ground three steps undersize because it has been severely weakened.

46. Examine the cam lobes and the cam followers on the pushrods for excessive wear. The cam could be reground or a new one could be installed. If ordering a new cam, look for the + or - number on the backside of the cam gear, such as +1, +2, -1, -2 or even 0. Be sure your new cam is the same. These markings are not over- and undersize, but use a different pitch of the cam gear teeth to accommodate adjusting of backlash between the crank gear and cam gear.

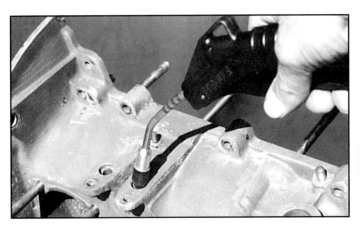

47. This section is one of the least technical but most important. Clean the case in a solvent tank and use the solvent spray hose to force solvent through all oil passages. Use a small gun barrel-type brush in all passages. Next, blow out all air passages with high pressure air while holding your hand over the outlets. Use a can of carburetor cleaner to spray into the passages along with more brushing. Follow up with a water hose and spray through all passages with more compressed air. Scrub the outside of the case with bristle brushes or wire brushes as necessary. Remove all gaskets carefully without gouging the case. Dry the whole case thoroughly with an air hose as magnesium corrodes if left wet. Take time and care cleaning; just a few pieces of grit is all it takes to destroy your new bearings.

48. Remove the copper crush gaskets from the intake ports, being careful not to gouge the sealing surface of the head; it could cause a vacuum leak after assembly.

49. Each cylinder on the 36 hp and early 40 hp uses a copper crush gasket on the cylinder and seals it against the cylinder head in a machined step groove. Commonly misunderstood, this is not a seal for compression. The top of the cylinder seats fully against the top of the combustion chamber for a compression seal. The copper gasket is a secondary seal added on to prevent carbon monoxide from getting into the heater boxes and interior of the car if the heads should loosen up. This heating system is referred to as the "stale air system." The "fresh air system" began in August 1962 on the 40 hp engine. It did not utilize heat from the cylinders, but from the exhaust header surface. This keeps carbon monoxide fumes from entering the car interior.

50. Check all valve adjustment screw tips and replace any that are uneven.

51. Here is the worn rod bearing getting very thin. It was beginning to squeeze out to the edges, where it could have reduced the rod side clearance and created a lot of heat, leading to seizure or breakage.

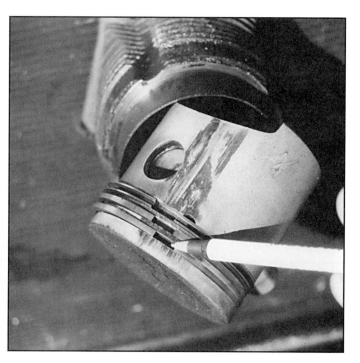

52. The last engine builder apparently didn't stagger the ring gaps, which caused compression flow and piston burning.

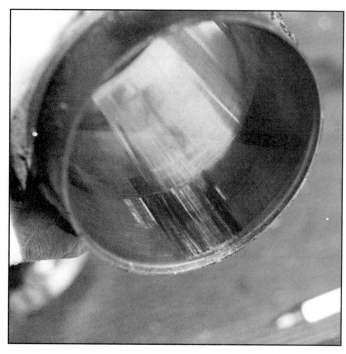

53. The cylinder also suffered severe scoring and compression blowby.

15 VINTAGE ENGINE REBUILD, PART II

Text & Photography by Hank Roed

1. The old crank was scrapped. Here is a freshly reground crank from BFY in Orange, California, along with rebuilt connecting rods from Rimco in Santa Ana They are laid out showing the position they will be installed, with the bearing tang notches and numbers at the bottom. This applies to all air-cooled VWs and Porsches regardless of the rods used.

In Chapter 14, we showed you how to identify and tear down a Volkswagen 36-hp engine With the engine now completely apart and all parts inspected for wear, we'll continue with Part II, which will show you how to assemble the short block. Our vintage engine rebuild continues in the next chapter with Part III, which will be installation of the pistons, cylinders, and heads. With everything nice and clean and all the parts you will need on hand, let's pick up where we left off and get the short block together.

2. A close-up of the bearing tang notches. Note where the rod and cap mate there is a slightly beveled edge. If the big end of the rod needed so much remachining that the bevel is gone, use a file or smooth stone grinder to recreate a slight bevel. The bevel prevents the back side of the bearing from being scraped on installation, which could cause the scrapings to get under the bearing and then seize on the crank when torqued.

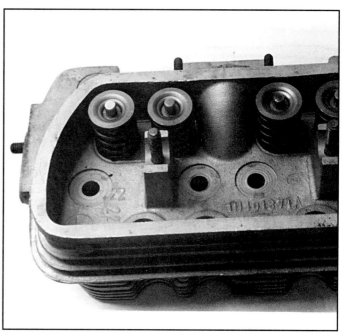

3. The 36 hp gland nut on the left is shorter than the later one on the right. The longer gland nut will bottom out in the 36 hp crank and will not hold onto the flywheel. Note the early gland nut has a bronze bushing with rifled bore. A later short nut has roller bearings as on the long one.

4. The cylinder heads were sent to Heads Up in Anaheim for a precision three-angle valve job, new valve guides and to make all valve stems of equal length. Only a few thousandths cut was required for the cylinder-seating surface. Please note that if a deep cut is made, an equal amount must be removed from the step for the copper gasket, otherwise it will prevent the head from sealing at the top of the cylinder.

5. After the case is thoroughly cleaned, the left half is installed in the engine stand. This engine case had never been line-bored and still looked good. There were no ridges in the main bearing saddles, and even the old bearings fit nice and snug. With the 0.010" under reground crank, we needed standard O.D. and 0.010" under I.D. bearings. These were not readily available. Although known for their big off-road engines, Johnson's Bug Machine in Santee, California, just happened to have a set. They were trial-inserted into the case without the crank, and fit fine.

6. The rod main journals on the reground and polished crank were checked then cleaned in solvent with wire brushes, which were run through all oil passages. After blowing dry with the air hose, a clean lint-free rag was used to clean all journals.

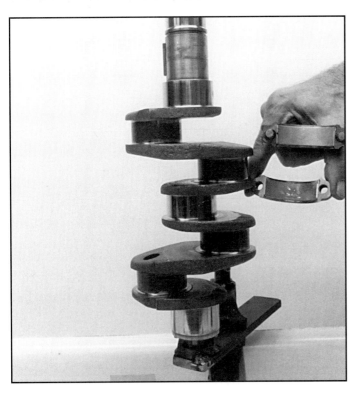

7. The new 0.010-inch undersize rod bearings are fitted to the rod and cap, then oiled.

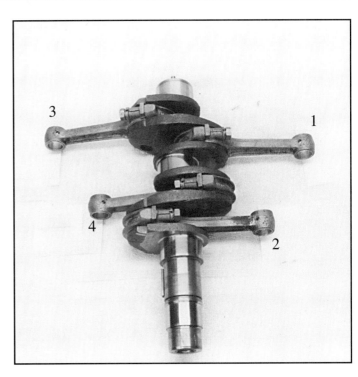

8. The rods and caps are installed on the crank finger-tight. All bearing tangs and numbers are matched as on the bottom, with number one rod at TDC as it will be in the engine. Tighten all rod bolts.

9. Check the rod side clearance with a feeler gauge. It should be 0.007" to 0.016". Also check that the rod gap is aligned with the rod by cocking the feeler gauge and moving it against the mating surfaces. If it catches on the edge, the cap is offset and will reduce your overall side clearance.

10. To correct a misaligned cap, tap the cap in the direction it needs to go then recheck with the feeler gauge. Torque the rods to 36 ft-lb with a 14mm socket. All rods should be able to fall free of their own weight without any sticky spots. If any rods stick, disassemble, clean thoroughly and try again. If not successful, the big end of the rod may not be machined correctly or, if you are using your old crank, a journal might be out of round.

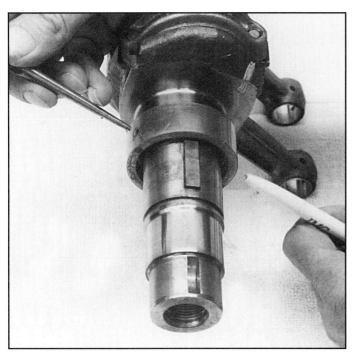

11. With the 40 hp and later engines, the way this bearing goes in is determined by an offset recessed hole that fits the dowel pin in the case. With the 36 hp and Porsche engines, the recess is centered. To determine which way to install the bearing, look at the oil galley holes in both case halves, and align them with the bearing oil holes as shown here with a pencil and scribe. Always use clean, fresh oil for assembly.

12. The steel cam drive gear goes with the chamfered edge towards the bearing. First check for burred teeth by meshing with the cam gear and rolling it all the way around

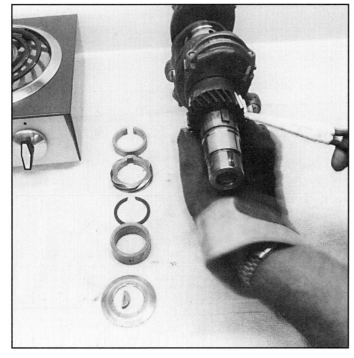

13. Heat the cam drive gear on a hot plate or in hot oil and slide it on. If it sticks before going all the way on, tap it with a drift punch while being careful not to hit the teeth.

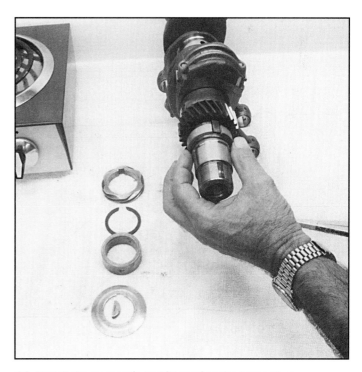

14. Install the spacer ring while testing the brass gear.

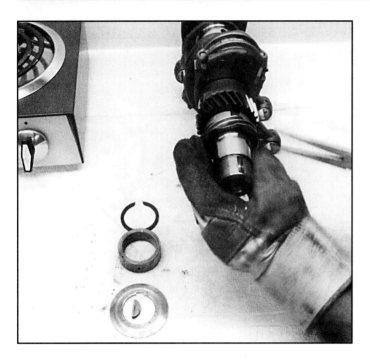

15. Position the brass gear, ensuring it's all the way on.

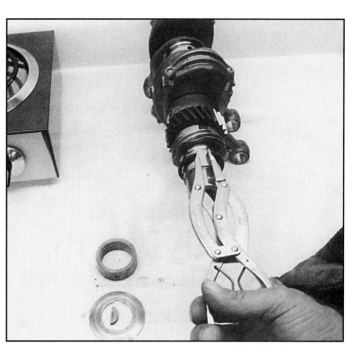

16. Install the snap ring with snap ring pliers and make sure it snaps completely into the groove.

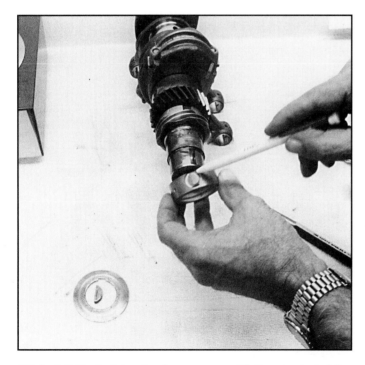

17. Install the last bearing in sequence with the opening of the groove on the side toward the snap ring.

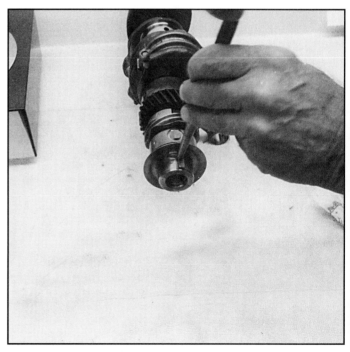

18. Install the oil slinger ring, ensuring the concave side faces away from the crank. Then include the woodruff key, tapping it in square and firm.

19. Check for missing or damaged oil sump studs. Install new ones as needed with red Locktite®. If the threads in the case are too loose, you can use a longer stud with a self-locking nut, such as a Nylock on the inside of the case. If the threads in the case are non-existent, you will need a special step stud that requires drilling and tapping or a Helicoil insert.

20. Here is the vacuum advance unit from the VJUR4BR8 distributor, which if functioning correctly, will give better gas mileage than a centrifugal-only distributor. Distributors in the VJU4BR8 range also incorporate centrifugal weights and work in conjunction with the vacuum advance to accommodate varying engine load. To correctly adjust the amount of vacuum advance, turn the threaded rod until it measures 1.709", plus or minus 0.008", to the vacuum chamber assembly housing. Shown here is a large adjusting nut and small jam nut. Loosen the jam nut and turn the large nut until it measures 0.138", plus or minus 0.006", to the vacuum chamber housing, and tighten the jam nut. The long hex-shaped section and nut on the outside of the canister houses an adjustable spring for the diaphragm, which is set at the factory with special tools. No attempt should be made to adjust it.

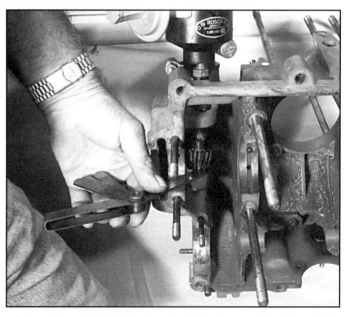

21. Install the small coil spring with a dab of grease into the distributor drive gear and install on the case with one thick or two thin thrust washers for a total thickness of approximately 0.050". Next, install the distributor, which has been cleaned and painted with the I.D. plate masked off.

22. While lifting up the distributor drive gear, pre-load it against the spring and check for approximately 0.100" or 1/8" clearance.

85

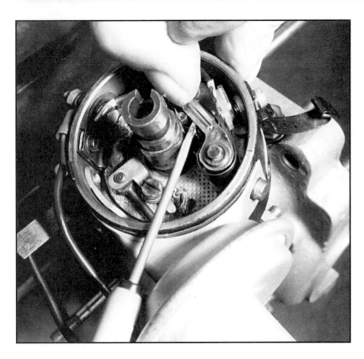

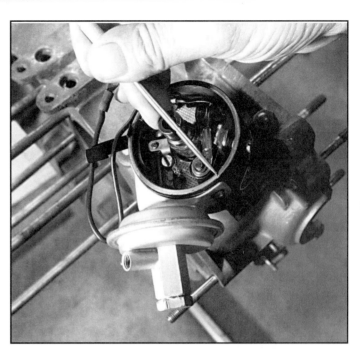

23. Install new points and set the gap to 0.016" while the rubbing block is on the peak of the distributor cam lobe. Apply Bosch grease to the cam lobes to the side of the rubbing block on the points. This way, as the rubbing block wears down, fresh grease is applied and the point gap will remain correct much longer.

24. Loosely attach the vacuum chamber to the distributor using a handmade thin cardboard gasket. Tighten the pull rod bracket screw and ground wire lead. Install the rotor and bring it in line with the mark on the edge of the distributor. In this position the points should have just started to open. It is best checked with a test light. If it is impossible to obtain this condition by shifting the vacuum chamber in the mounting screw holes, the length of the pull rod should be altered and the nut readjusted to 0.138", plus or minus 0.006". Then tighten the screws.

25. Oil the pushrods and check that none will bind on the cam follower guide plates; they should fall free of their own weight. Shown here is one that was sticking. Also try rotating the push rod. There should be no discernable clearance due to the flat side. Factory tolerance is quite close at 0.0004" to 0.0008".

26. The sticking cam follower was adjusted until it would fall free. After unfolding the lock tab, the guide plate was adjusted.

27. The adjustment is done laterally and care must be taken when re-tightening the nut not to let the guide plate twist. If twisted, the flat seal will guide the cam follower face crooked on the cam shaft lobes, resulting in high wear. Lastly, fold back and lock the tab.

28. Replace all four dowel pins in the left-hand case and one in the right. Insert the center main split bearings in both case halves with the oil holes corresponding to each other.

29. Oil the rear main bearing and slide it onto the crank with the dowel-pin locating hole closest to the flywheel.

30. With the distributor in place and rotor pointing to the number one position notch on the rim, pick up the crank as shown by number one and two connecting rods.

31. Gently insert the crank into place while holding it up slightly by the number one rod; you will be able to rotate the rear main bearing and feel when it lines up with the dowel pin. Then gently lay the rod down without dinging the case sealing surface.

32. Repeat the process holding the number two rod and engage the other bearings on the dowel pins.

33. With a soft mallet, tap gently along the crank but do not hit any bearings All bearings should now be firmly in place, and because you were holding up the number one rod with the distributor rotor at the number one mark, you will have closely engaged the timing.

34. Coat all journals and lobes on the cam with cam lube. Rotate the crank a few degrees clockwise and you will see the two dots on the cam drive gear. The 36 hp does not use cam bearings; so, while holding the cam, engage the timing on the face of the cam gear between the two dots on the crank gear. While keeping the teeth engaged, roll the cam down into the case. If you ever need to change a cam gear, note it goes with the dot in line with the slot in the cam.

35. First rotate the crank clockwise by the rods and feel for binding between the gears. Next slowly rotate the crank counterclockwise. All should turn freely. If the cam tries to climb up out of the case you will need a –1 or –2 etc. These numbers are on the back side of the cam gear. None means it's a zero. If there is no binding, check the backlash by holding the cam down and rocking the cam gear. It should barely be perceptible, as the factory spec is 0.004" to 0.0014". The only other alternatives to correct backlash might be to use a different gear on the crank. Just remember to use 36 hp gears, as the degree of pitch is less than on later engines.

36. Coat the cam plug with sealant. Put some sealant in the groove of the case but not on the journal. Insert the cam plug.

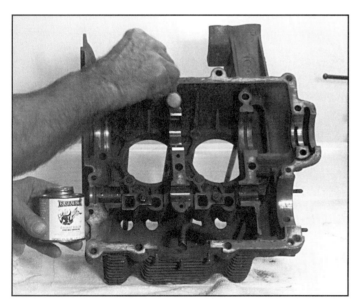

37. Coat the entire perimeter of the right case half, the cam plug groove and the six holes for the studs with sealant. Be careful not to get any near the smaller oil passage holes. I use Gasgacinch® or Aviation Permatex. Others are your choice, but do not use a silicone type. It could squeeze out into the engine and plug oil passages

38. Before the case sealant dries too much, press the rods sideways or have someone hold them and set the right case half down on the studs. Tap around the case with a mallet. Be sure the cam plug is still in place.

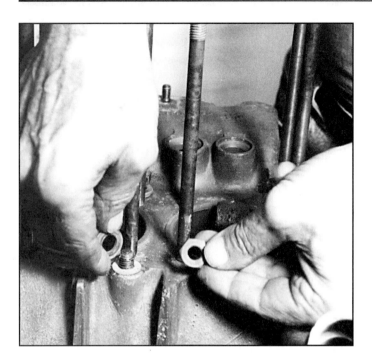

39. At the six main case studs apply sealant, the paper washer, metal washer and nuts.

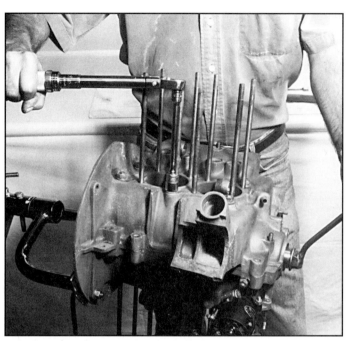

40. Torque the six main case nuts to about seven ft-lb working from the center studs outward. At the same time, rotate the crank and stop if anything begins to bind. Here I use a pulley nut welded to a cylinder head stud, or you could temporarily slip on the pulley. If any main bearings are not centered in the dowel pins, you will crush the bearing and ruin it; definitely not desired with hard-to-find bearings. Finally, torque the six main nuts evenly to 22 ft-lb while turning the crank.

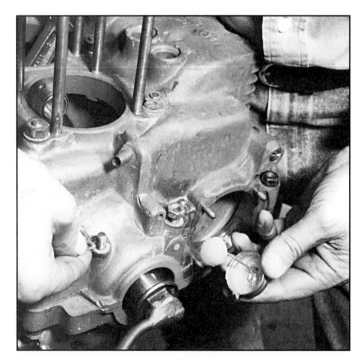

41. Install all nuts and washers around the perimeter of the case, using paper washers and sealant on the ones shown here. Do not fully torque them yet, especially the ones near the oil pump.

42. Tighten the two bolts at the cam plug.

43. Put a dab of grease in the cam slot.

44. There are two O.D. pump gaskets, one thick and one thin. The thick one goes on first. Use a sealant, but please no silicone or it may plug the oil passage.

45. Check the clearance between the gears and oil pump without a gasket. The factory spec is no more than 0.004". Closer to zero is better and would improve oil pressure. After the gasket is in place, the clearance will be sufficient.

46. Install the oil pump housing, put some assembly lube on the gears and shaft, and coat both sides of the thin gasket with a thin sealant. Again, no silicone! The factory recommends leaving these gaskets dry or wetting them with oil.

47. The cover plate must be absolutely flat. A piece of wet or dry sandpaper on a glass surface works well for resurfacing. Just be sure it's cleaned afterward and, with a little assembly lube in the center of the cover plate, install it. The same copper washers as are on an oil strainer plate will work here to prevent leaks. Torque the nut to no more than 5 ft-lb.

48. Turn the engine upside down and squirt some oil in the oil pressure relief valve hole. Install the plunger with the hollow side toward you and check that it moves freely with a magnet, bent wire or screwdriver.

49. Check that the spring is 52–53mm or 2.05–2.09" and install it into the hollow of the plunger. Finally, tighten the plug with a copper gasket using a square-shank screwdriver and crescent wrench; tighten it to crush the gasket.

50. Install a clean oil strainer with a dry paper gasket on each side and cover the plate. Be sure the cover plate is flat inside, as the six holes are sometimes deformed from over-tightening. Install the copper washers and torque the nuts to five ft-lb.

VINTAGE ENGINE REBUILD, PART III

16

Text & Photography by Hank Roed

1. Setting the crankshaft endplay requires three shims available in varying thickness. They are a smaller diameter than later engines. Install the paper gaskets dry on the dowels.

From 1954 through 1960, the Volkswagen Bug came from the factory with a 64mm stroke by 77mm bore, 1192cc 36 hp engine by S.A.E. testing. In European rating, it was a 36 hp D.I.M. Compared to most cars on the road of that era, it was a real wimp, but that's the way Volkswagen intended it. They knew the simplest, most inexpensive way to get long engine life to match the sturdy chassis and body was deliberately restrict the performance of the engine. Part III of the Vintage Engine Rebuild continues with final assembly techniques, right up to bolting on the heads. Parts I and II are Chapters 14 and 15, respectively.

2. If the teeth on the flywheel are ragged, now is a good time to file them clean at an angle evenly all around. If available, turn them on a lathe; the material is soft. An alternative would be to have a hardened steel gear pressed on. This service is offered on an exchange basis by Gene Berg Enterprises (Orange, Calif.) with your choice of a 6- or 12-volt ring gear.

3. There are several methods of setting end play. Here the paper gasket and original three shims are installed, minus the flywheel seal and the gland nut torqued down to a temporary 75 ft-lb. A dial indicator is clamped to the case and the flywheel pushed towards the case. Set the indicator on zero then pull the flywheel outward. The desired end play is 0.003 to 0.005" with 0.006" inches being the wear limit. It can be adjusted with different thickness shims exchanged. Use a micrometer to measure the shims and substitute thicker or thinner shims as necessary, but use a total of three shims.

4. Remove the flywheel and with the now-correct shim stack in place and the paper gasket coat the outer edge of the seal with a thin sealant and when tacky, insert the seal. It can be tapped in with a mallet but may go crooked and get out of round. Your VW parts house may be able to get you a seal installer such as this.

5. Using a seal installer, screw the shank into the flywheel and tighten the nut with a wrench or continuously tighten by hand as you tap around the edges. The seal will bottom out in the case when approximately flush. On later engines, it will be recessed below the case surface. Coat the lip of the seal with oil.

6. Be sure you have the short gland nut and wavy washer. Install the flywheel on the crank dowel pins and snug up the gland nut.

7. With two bolts in the flywheel, arrange a steel bar or angle iron as shown and you can easily torque down the gland nut to the 217 lb-ft of final torque.

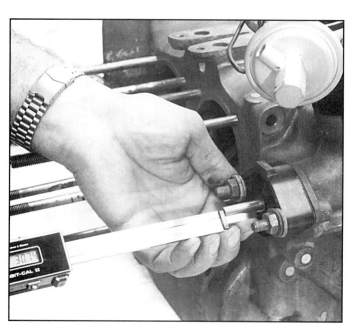

8. The stroke of the fuel pump rod can be measured by lightly bolting on the spacer block with one gasket and turning the crank. The stroke should be about 4mm or 0.160". There is a more precise method but it requires VW Gauge 328. The stroke is only half of the equation. The other half is how close the fuel pump is to the engine. Factory-required pump pressure is only 1.3 to 1.85 psi with the carburetor needle valve closed and the engine at 1000 to 3000 rpm. Pressure can be reduced by adding gaskets and increased by shaving the spacer block.

9. Always remove and install pistons from the bottom of the cylinder. Wash the pistons and cylinders in clean solvent and blow-dry with compressed air. Keep each piston with the cylinder it came from.

10. Lay the pistons and cylinders out in order on your bench. Note there is an arrow on top and a bump inside the piston at the wrist pin boss. Both of these indicate that they go towards the flywheel. Ring gaps and side clearance rarely need to be checked when using a new matching set. If you plan on re-ringing the old pistons and honing the cylinders, the ring gaps are 0.012" to 0.017" on all rings. On the compression ring, the side clearance is 0.0014 to 0.0022 inches with a wear limit of 0.008".

11. Upon assembly, you will be inserting the wrist pins from the outboard ends, so now install a circlip on the inboard side of each piston.

12. Remember the photo of all the ring gaps lined up and the scorched piston during disassembly? We don't want that to happen again, so set the lower oil control ring up to the top at the 12 o'clock position, the middle oil scraper ring at 4 o'clock and the top compression ring at 8 o'clock. Here, I use a HAZET split-type 77mm ring compressor, but adjustable ones will also work. Note the number one and two wrist pins partially inserted and piston arrow towards the flywheel.

13. Oil all the wrist pin bushings in the rods and push in the wrist pin. If they are snug, use a wrist pin driver to tap in slowly, but don't dislodge the previously installed circlip at the other end.

14. Install the outboard wrist pin circlip.

15. Install the paper gaskets on each cylinder with a thin coat of sealant. This is one of the places on a VW engine where heat-proof real silicone sealant can be used, but is normally reserved for stroked engines with metal spacers and no gaskets. It is also difficult to use as it dries fast and thick, requiring a fast assembly; four cylinders' pushrod tubes and the cylinder heads must be torqued down before it gets too thick.

16. With some clean oil on a clean lint-free cloth, wipe the inside of the barrels thoroughly and you will see some dirt picked up by the cloth, even though you cleaned them. This will also leave enough oil on the cylinder bore to prevent scratching the new rings. Leave the rings dry and they will break in properly.

17. Offer the cylinder to the piston and tap on the cylinder with your open palm while watching the rings to ensure they don't pop out from the ring compressor until sliding inside the cylinder. A flywheel lock may be necessary.

18. Continue inserting the wrist pin from outboard of the cylinders as shown here on the number two cylinder. Remember to stagger ring gaps and arrows toward the flywheel.

19. Sometimes a cylinder may be too tight in the case. Never tap on top of the cylinder to coax it in. You have a very thin rim at the top, which must be true and flat to seal against the head. If coaxing is necessary, use a soft piece of wood like a piece of a pine 2x4 and tap on it instead.

20. After all the cylinders are on, check the deck height with a depth gauge reading at the center of the piston. No factory specs seem to be available, but 0.050" to 0.070" should do. Mainly, you're checking for variations such as a cylinder not seated, a rod of different length, or double gaskets, etc. If all the pistons stick out of the cylinders, it's your lucky day, as you may have an Okrasa stroker crank. Under such happy circumstances, have spacers machined to fit under the barrels to restore deck clearance.

21. With a straightedge, check that the cylinders are even. If a cylinder is cocked, it may have some old gasket material under it or need to be tapped down to equal level.

22. Press the cylinder air deflector plates into the studs under the cylinders on both sides.

23. Carefully install all pushrod tube seals by pulling on from one side. Pushing them straight on will, at times, cause a cut from the sharp edge of the pushrod tube.

24. Some say dry, some say oiled, but I have always had the best luck applying Gaskacinch to all the seals.

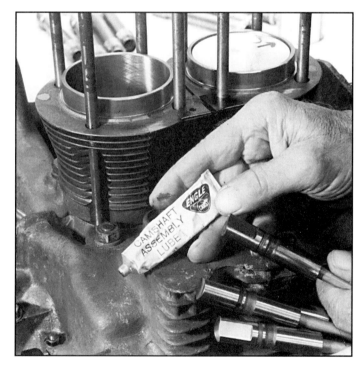

25. Coat the lifters with cam lube and install them. Also, put some cam lube on the rocker arm end of the pushrods.

26. With the pushrods in place, install one copper gasket on each cylinder with the split side of the gasket towards the cylinder head.

27. Here is the welded seam on the pushrod tube, which should be turned to face the top of the engine.

28. Apply a thin coating of high temp silicone sealant to the four washers for the lower cylinder head studs.

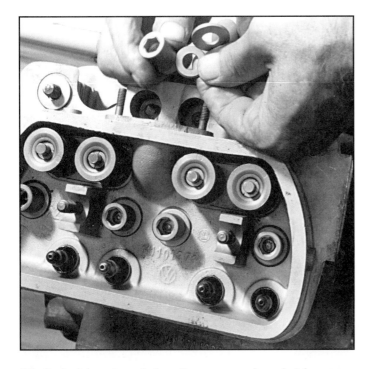

29. Sealant is not needed on the upper washers, but be sure a washer isn't stuck in the recessed holes. The four recessed holes take a washer with a smaller O.D.

30. With anti-seize compound applied to the threads, torque down the lower row of nuts to 7 lb-ft, starting in the center and alternating left to right for an even seating of the head. Then use the same procedure on the top nuts. Do both heads. Now torque the heads to 27 lb-ft, starting at the lower center and crisscrossing top to bottom while working your way outboard. Recheck all nuts for final torque.

VINTAGE ENGINE REBUILD, PART IV

17

Text & Photography by Hank Roed

1. The unique 36 hp rocker assembly half-apart for reference. After taking it all apart, inspect the end clips and washers for wear. Also, check the shaft and polish it. I used a discarded crankshaft polishing belt. The rocker arms can be cleaned in carb dip and the OD passages blown clear. Reassemble with assembly lube or cam lube.

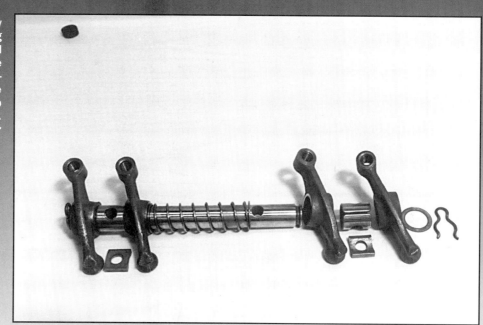

Part IV of the Vintage Engine Rebuild continues with more final assembly techniques, right up to final installation in the engine. During final assembly, it is essential that you make sure the environment you are working in is impeccably clean. Dirt and debris can wreak havoc on the inside of the engine, even minor amounts. Parts I, II and III are Chapters 14, 15 and 16 respectively, in case you turned to this section first. If you've been faithfully following along, your hard work is about to come together!

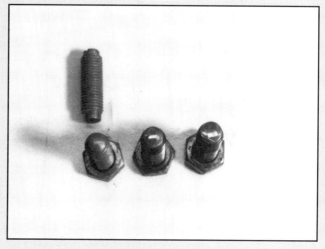

2. Inspect the valve adjustment screws. From left to right is new, OK and marginal. Replace as necessary.

3. Check the adjustment screw to the valve stem alignment. It should be slightly off-center, so each valve opening and closing causes the screw to rotate the valve for more even wear at the seat. Shown here are the screws too far left of the valve stem. With additional washers and patience this can be corrected.

4. This is how the adjusting screw-to-valve stem alignment should look with a slight off-center alignment.

5. Install the half round caps on the rocker shaft studs and evenly torque to 14 ft-lb. Turn the crankshaft until the distributor rotor points to the notch on the distributor, and the crank pulley notch is in line with the case halves at the top. This is number one TDC. Make a mark at the bottom of the pulley and adjust the valves to 0.004" on the number one cylinder. Turn the crank counterclockwise half a turn, so the mark you made on the bottom is now on top, and adjust the valves for the number two cylinder. Continue the same way for numbers three and four cylinders.

6. A caution note on powdercoating sheet metal: Here the powdercoating company didn't tape the pulley grooves completely. The remaining powdercoat is thick enough to rub against the bore in the case and could do harm—by leaking or binding. This pulley was not usable.

7. Using the double-lock nut method, bad or missing exhaust studs can be changed, but first apply Red Locktite® to the threads that go into the head.

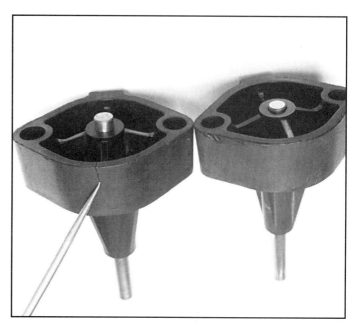

8. Check the fuel pump block for cracks; many become cracked by folks who try to cure oil leaks by over-tightening things.

9. Install the crankshaft pulley sheet metal and pulley, then torque the bolt to 85 ft-lb.

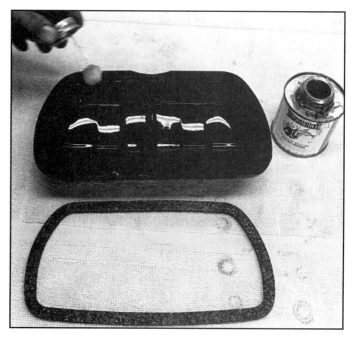

10. Coat one side of the valve cover gasket and the lip in the valve cover with sealant, and let it become tacky before joining the two glued sections to each other. When installing the valve covers, the tacky gasket will not slip out of place. Never use sealant against the cylinder head.

11. & 12. Install the two oil-cooler seals and tighten the three nuts and washers. You should upgrade from the original nuts at this location and use Nylock nuts. They have a nylon insert that grips the threads and won't work loose.

 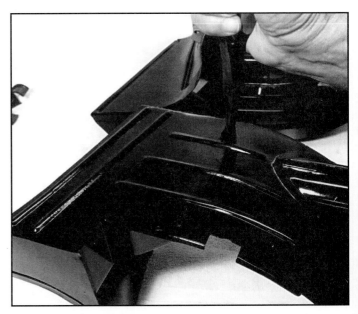

13. Each of the heater control flaps has two tabs that ride in the slots shown. This tab was broken off and a piece was welded back on. The curved bracket is for the pull rod.

14. Here is why many tabs may be found broken. They are secured with a slight twist on the outside of the heater channels.

15. Attach the thermostat bracket. The thermostat bolt can be left loose at this stage, as it will be checked for adjustment after the air control ring is installed.

16. Place the cylinder head cover on numbers one and two cylinders, which are not shown here for a more clear illustration. Install the air control ring shaft and mounting assembly with return spring and thermostat control arm, seen lying on the cylinder head.

17. The control arm connects to the thin rod coming up from the thermostat at the space in the cylinder head fins. Check for any interference.

18. The straight end of the coil spring points up and could interfere with the fan shroud installation later. The end of the shaft takes a horseshoe clip in a groove and the control arm clamping nuts are left loose for now.

19. Install the heater channels while checking that they fit properly between the case and cylinder head. Secure them with screws from the top.

20. Slip the generator backing plate on, along with the retainer ring. The folded edge of the ring goes toward the generator.

21. Install the woodruff key, fan hub and flat spacer on the generator shaft.

22. Between the spacer and fan, shims can be added or subtracted to attain correct backing plate clearance.

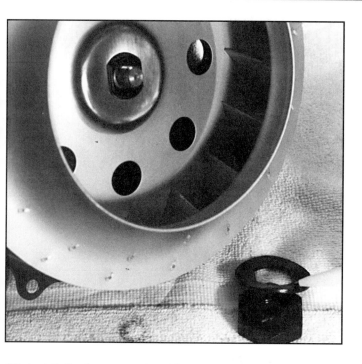

23. Install the fan, any extra shims, and the wavy lock washer shown. Tighten the nut snugly for now.

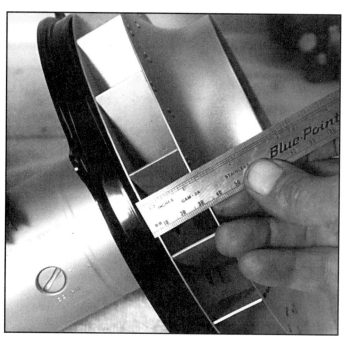

24. Check the fan-to-backing plate clearance for 1.8mm or 0.070" approximate. Spin the fan to check runout. If not true, find the spot of most clearance and tap the fan with a mallet. Keep checking until the fan runs true.

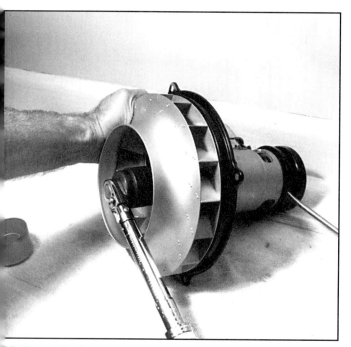

25. Torque the fan nut to 43 ft-lb. Note the screwdriver in the pulley slot to prevent turning.

26. Place the fan in the fan shroud and tighten the four bolts with a 10mm socket wrench. Do not use sheet metal screws here as usually they won't be tight enough and will vibrate loose.

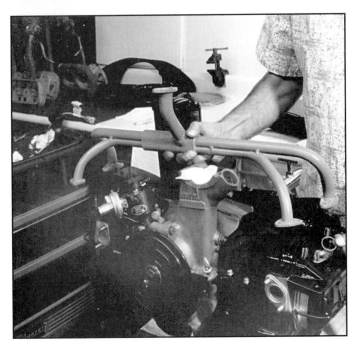

27. Place the intake port copper gaskets in place with the split part toward the head and install the manifold and four nuts, but leave them loose for now. Before painting the manifold, check to ensure the heat riser passages are not clogged up. They can be burned out with an oxy-acetylene torch and lots of banging about. Another method is using an old clutch cable in an electric drill. Both ways are very tedious. Finding clear ones may be easier, check the large passages also. Check all parts that have access to the inside of the engine for debris.

28. The hole in the generator stand is open to the inside of the engine, and the oil can flow out the top. A thin gasket must be made to fit this opening. Use gasket material and cut it a bit over-size because it can shrink with age, and it can slip a little when installing or changing the generator. If the case surface is a bit corroded, as sometimes happens, use a thin coat of a thick sealant.

29. With the new gasket in place on the generator stand, install the fan shroud and generator assembly. Install the two-fan shroud hold-down bolts and washers loosely and then install the generator clamp and tighten it. Spin the fan a last time to check for interference.

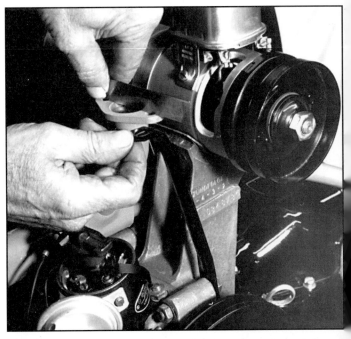

30. Check that the carburetor flange is straight, as they are sometimes bent from having too many gaskets and over-torquing.

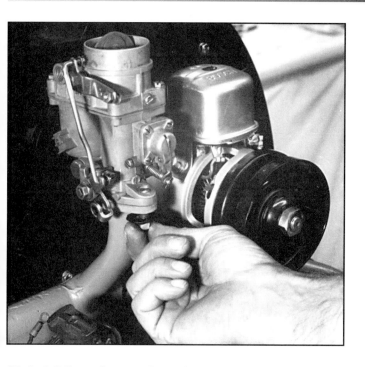

31. Install the carburetor along with the manifold-to-case brace. Leave loose for now.

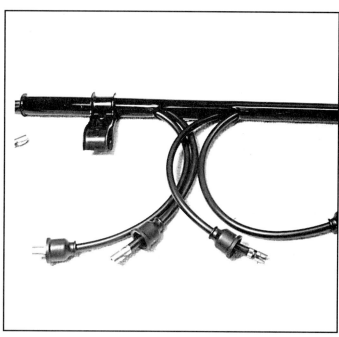

32. After removing the seals, push the ignition wires through the loom; long wires to cylinders one and two and short wires to three and four. Loosely place the ignition wire loom clamps in place and put the seals back on the ignition wires.

33. Install the loom on the engine and tighten the clamp onto the intake manifold

34. Install the coil and bracket and shiny new Bosch decal. Defying logic, note it is upside down. It is meant to be read correctly when the coil is turned the other way, as it would be when sitting on a shelf. It was better connected after being brought to my attention. From experience, the decal requires an additional dab of adhesive and a light coat of clear Krylon to prevent the ink from fading.

35. When installing the distributor cap, be sure this half round notch goes over the insulating washer at the distributor wire lead.

36. By pushing and pulling the ignition wires in the loom, you can correctly connect number one plug to number one in the distributor cap, which is in line with the mark on the rim of the distributor. Follow through counterclockwise at the top of the cap with numbers two, three and four.

37. Install the heater junction boxes. Note the control rod in my right hand. The junction boxes should be refinished in heat-resistant dull gray or semi-flat paint.

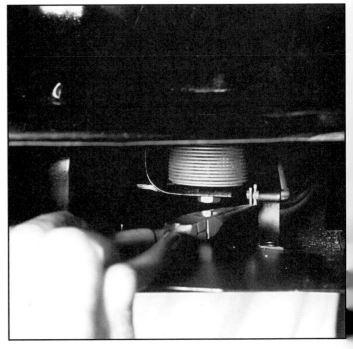

38. Insert the control rod into the flapper arm and secure with a cotter pin.

39. Tighten the header pipe to the cylinder head and the bolt on the bottom that joins the heater channel and junction box. Check the control flaps for free movement.

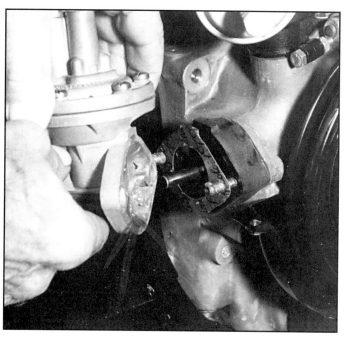

40. Check the fuel pump flange with a straight edge and pack the recess with universal grease. Install a gasket on both sides of the fuel pump spacer block with a thin coat of sealant. Match the tab on the gasket with the fuel pump and spacer block. The tab goes up.

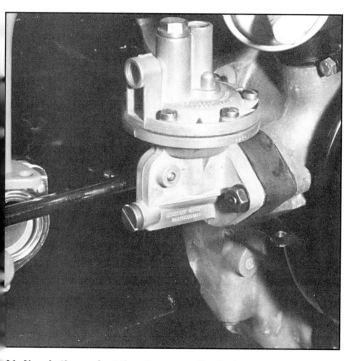

41. Now is the easiest time to access the fuel pump nuts. The factory torque spec is not given. It says "tighten, but do not over-tighten." Over-tightening will crack the fuel pump spacer block. A good rule of thumb is to snug down, then go 1/4 turn past that point.

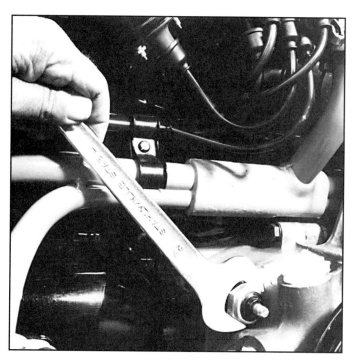

42. Install the oil pressure warning switch. The later switches used a push-on spade terminal, but the '54 Oval this engine is going into has an all-new original style electrical harness, and so here the correct screw-type terminal is used on an NOS oil pressure switch.

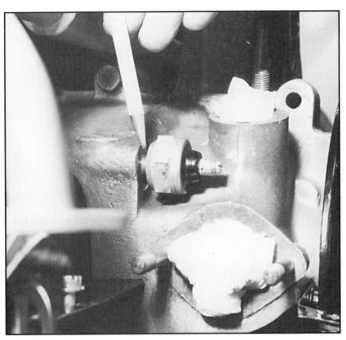

43. The oil pressure switch has a tapered thread. The more you turn it in, the more it wedges outward on the case. A common mistake is made when this switch is cranked up flush up against the case. This pre-loads the case so severely, that during a hot-running condition, the case can crack and lose oil pressure. Leave space as shown here. If the case threads are worn, try using blue Locktite Lock & Seal, just a little on the threads, not in the oil gallery. Teflon tap will also work, but it is so slippery, it will feel loose and give a false sense of being in far enough. Don't ruin your engine over such a simple thing. Insert the sheet metal piece under the fuel pump and loosely attach with one sheet metal screw.

44. Slip the muffler onto the header tubes and cylinder heads.

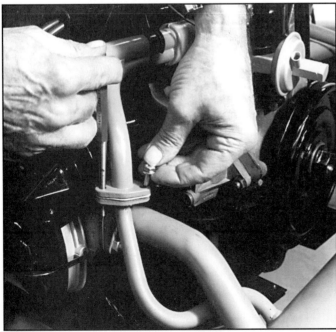

45. Insert the muffler and heat riser gaskets and use a drift punch to align the heat riser and install the bolts loosely.

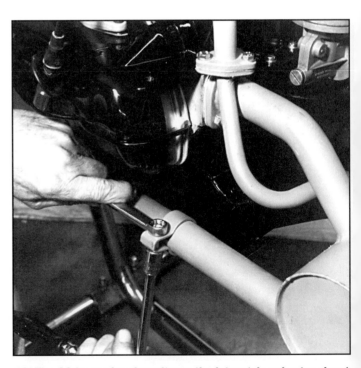

46. The 36 hp engine doesn't use the later-style asbestos donut gaskets and clamps. It uses a simple slip fit and clamp as shown. Please, no American muffler clamps here as they crush and distort the tubes.

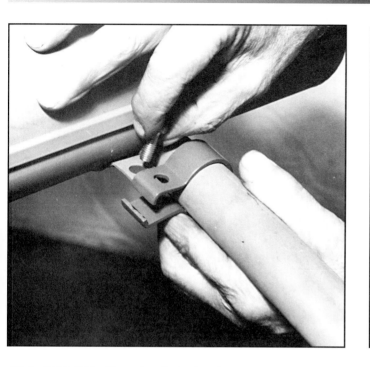

47. In 1954, VW still used a single tip tailpipe clamped the same as the header pipes, plus a bracket on the muffler.

48. Remember all those nuts, bolts and screws we left loose? Now they can all be tightened. Start with the intake manifold, alternating torque to squeeze down evenly onto the copper crush gaskets.

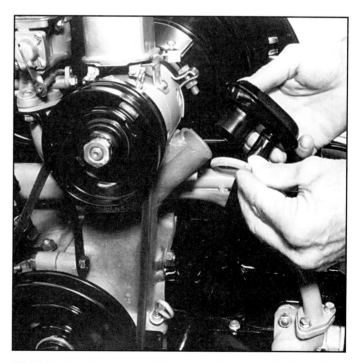

49. Now the carburetor and carburetor brace can be tightened, along with the heat riser bolts.

50. Up to 1954, VWs used this rather strange method of adding oil: an integral breather housing and road draft tube with no oil cap or tab to screw onto the case.

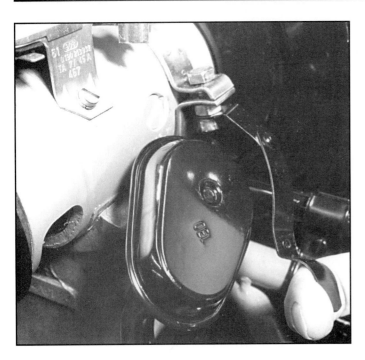

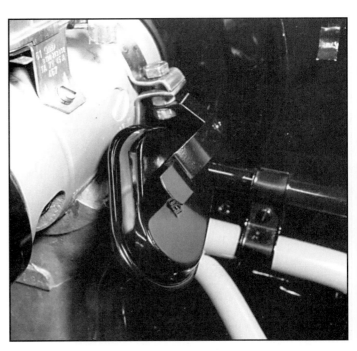

51. The method of holding it in place was a spring steel clip and bracket attached to the generator clamp that rests in a dipstick in the housing and is pivoted away so the housing can be lifted out of the oil-filler hole in the case. A rubber grommet slides on the neck to seal it. In 1955 it was similar, but had a tab to screw onto the case permanently and a regular oil cap. Both styles use a rubber grommet on the road draft tube to sheet metal junction.

52. Here is the spring steel clip in place. If you have this setup, be forewarned, as the generator strap and bracket position are crucial to a tight fit. Mount the bracket on the bottom of the generator strap and adjust positions; however, do not attempt to bend or tweak on the spring or bracket as it will break easily.

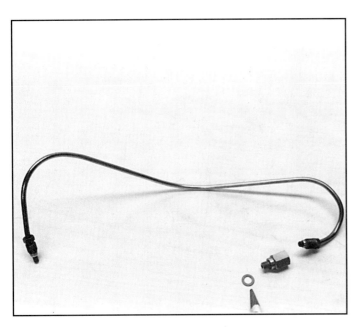

53. This is the metal distributor vacuum line. The adapter and crush washer on the right go to the carburetor. Both ends of the line have tapered sleeves to seal air tight, but the gasket is required between the adapter and carburetor. The gasket is one of a few you won't receive in a gasket kit, but a spare oil sump copper gasket works well If you have a centrifugal distributor, the carburetor must be plugged at the adapter fitting to prevent a severe intake vacuum leak!

54. Blow through the fuel lines to clear them and install at carburetor and fuel pump. They may need to be bent a little to prevent cross-threading. The inlet line to the fuel pump must have a rubber grommet where it passes through the sheet metal or the sharp sheet metal will wear through the soft copper fuel line, causing fuel leaks, engine stoppage, or a big ball of flames! By my thumb is the vacuum advance line at the distributor. It snakes around behind and to the right rear of the carburetor. Be careful not to cross-thread it.

55. All 36 hp engines originally came with an annular venturi-style thermostat and controlled air-regulating ring at the fan shroud air inlet. Many are missing, at least on the West Coast. Perhaps this is because someone thought it was unnecessary in a warm climate or didn't understand how it worked and/or how to adjust it, and just threw the dang thing away. Leaving it in place and adjusting it properly will extend the life of your engine by assisting it to reach operating temperature sooner. The S.A.E (Society of Automotive Engineers) showed the predominant cause of wear in any reciprocating engine is during starting and warm up. When adjusting, remember two things: 1) During assembly, the cold setting is closed and lightly preloaded against a rubber stop at the fan shroud (the rubber stop shown is temporary for testing, not original). 2) With the engine hot enough for the copper bellows thermostat to expand out to the top of the mounting bracket stop, the lip of the air ring should be 20mm or .79" from the top lip of the fan shroud. The adjustment is made at the control arm clamp using a 10mm wrench as shown here. If an adjustment error is made and the ring opens too far before the thermostat bracket limits travel, it will make contact with the spinning fan along with a horrible screeching and grinding noise. Maybe that's another reason so many are missing. Adjust it properly. Check that the bellows hits the top stop or the bracket with the air ring at a 20mm distance, and enjoy the extra longevity of your engine. The thermostat can also be checked in water heated from 149° to 158° F: It should then measure 46mm, or 1.8 inches.

56. Install the clutch disc with an alignment tool such as this old pilot shaft. At the pencil are tabs, which center the pressure plate inside the flywheel. If not careful, one could catch the edge of the flywheel and warp the clutch when the bolts are fully tightened.

57. Draw the pressure plate in evenly by alternating turning the bolts in a little at a time in a crisscross pattern.

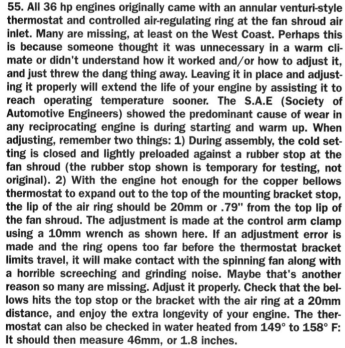

58. Torque the clutch bolts in a crisscross pattern to 25 ft-lbs. Check that the throwout bearing release plate is parallel to the flywheel.

59. With the starter half of a transmission housing, a starter, battery, gas, jumper cables and a hot wire to the coil, you can run your engine.

60. Here the engine is fitted to the restored '54 pan at West Coast Classics, with the '54 oval body in the background.

61. Here is the completed engine in a restored 1954 Beetle.

REPLACING THE ENGINE COMPARTMENT SEAL

18

Text & Photography by D.E. Meyers

1. Most VWs that are used as daily transportation run around with cracked and broken engine compartment seals.

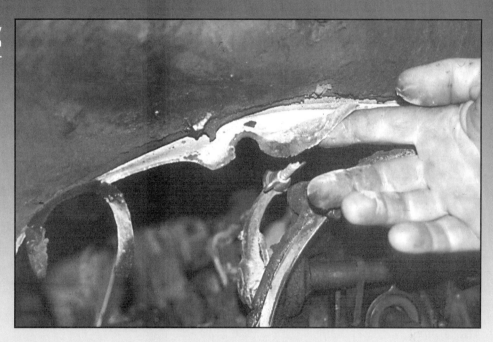

In the last four chapters, you've learned how to rebuild a 36 hp engine. No doubt, you're in a rush to get that engine back into the car and running. But before you do, check the engine compartment seal, and if it is worn at all, take the opportunity to replace it now. The seal can only be replaced while the engine is out of the car.

The engine compartment seal is that little piece of rubber that runs all around the engine compartment and makes a weatherproof seal between the engine compartment area of the body and the engine tin. Because the VW engine is cooled by air, it is important to have this seal in place, and in good condition.

The only items that you'll need are: a large screwdriver, a pair of cutters, a small wire brush, and some silicone spray. Silicone spray will make the seal slippery so it will slide through the channel it fits in.

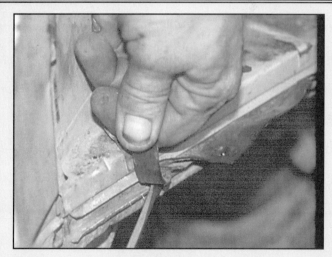

2. Pull, cut or dig the old seal out of the channel.

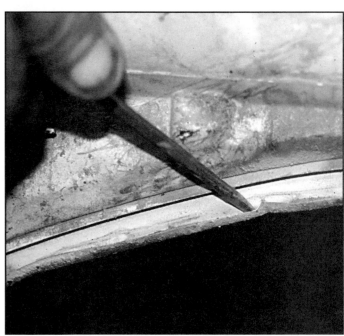

3. Clean out the channel with a small screwdriver and a wire brush. The cleaner the channel, the easier the new rubber will go in.

4. Use a screwdriver to straighten out any dents in the channel. This will allow the new rubber to slide in place much easier.

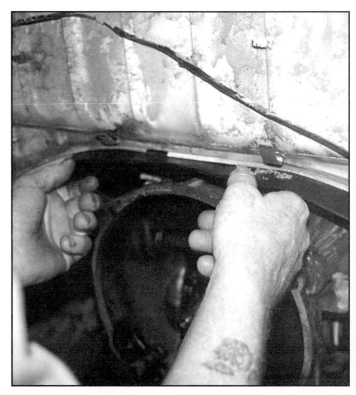

5. Spray the entire piece of new rubber with silicone spray. This too will make what would otherwise be an aggravating job easy.

6. Start the new rubber in one end of the channel, pulling and pushing it, working it through to the other end.

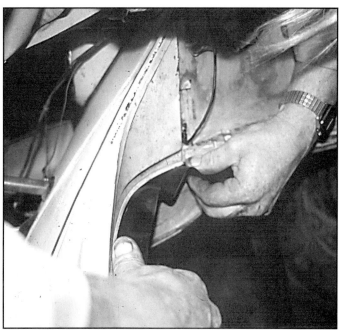

7. Run each end of the side pieces of rubber past the end of the channel about an inch or two and then cut the rest off.

8. Work the main piece of rubber along the rear channel of the engine compartment. Do each section in one complete piece.

9. At times, you may need to use a screwdriver to help work the rubber through the channel (be careful that you don't cut the rubber).

19

36 HP ENGINE TUNEUP

Text & Photography by Dave Cormack

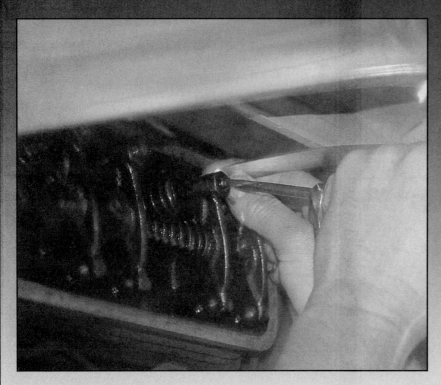

1. Just like later engines, the valves should be adjusted cold. The lifters and pushrods are in one piece and actually have wood inserts in them. Valve adjustment is critical on aircooled VWs, and George set the valves on this engine to 0.004".

Having been the only engine Volkswagen offered for many years and the long-time mainstay of the VW engine lineup, the 36-hp engine helped create part of the "bulletproof" reputation of Volkswagen powerplants. Under normal circumstances, they didn't give much trouble, and when properly maintained, the 36 hp would last for thousands of miles. In fact, before the rpm reached self-destruct levels, the little 28 PIC carb effectively acted like a governor, starving the car of fuel and air. Millions were built from 1953 to 1960, and there are still quite a few around today. Most Ovals or early Big Window Sedans, as well as countless Type IIs, used this powerplant. You can always tell a 25-, 30- or 36-horsepower engine by the generator stand, which is an integral part of the right side (cylinders number one and two) of the crankcase. With the increasing popularity of restored vintage

VWs, there are more of these engines popping up at VW car shows all the time. While there was a time that the only people who wanted 36-horse engine cases were the desert guys—who burned them to light up their camp—they are now quite desirable. If you have an Oval, and you don't have the correct year engine, then you can either hope to get lucky or expect to pay the price for a useable case. I decided to take the old '55 Sunroof up to a Der Kleiner Panzers 111 (DKP 111) meeting, a drive of about 75 miles. Along the way, I noticed that it just didn't seem to have the beans that it used to. While the 75,000-original-mile unit performed flawlessly, it just didn't feel like it should. It was time for a tune-up. I took the car to Escondido Foreign Car Service in Escondido, Calif., for a tune-up and an oil change. Owner George Lyra has been doing this type of work for 30 years now, and when he came to work for

Escondido Foreign car, anything he didn't know about VWs was taught to him by the previous owner, Fred Holterman, who used to work at the VW factory in Wolfsburg, so there is a remote chance that Fred actually helped build this '55! Fred has since retired and passed the baton on to George. I normally don't let anyone touch my pride and joy, but George is an exception. In fact, when I have a problem that I can't figure out, either on one of my aircoolers or the Jetta, George is one of the first people I call for help. His experience in this field cannot be faulted, and he has rebuilt literally hundreds of engines—many of them 36 horsepower units. The engine starts quicker (always a plus with a six-volt electrical system), runs smoother and is getting better fuel economy. It really doesn't take that long, and the task is easily within reach of a novice mechanic.

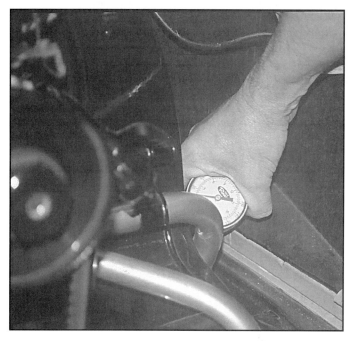

2. Next, the compression was checked to see if we had worse problems than a tune-up. The manual calls for 100 to 114 lb of compression pressure; we were fortunate to find ours all in that range. If you have one or more cylinders below about 90 lb, then a tune-up won't do much good. Important: Make sure you have the big wire from the ignition coil to the distributor cap unplugged!

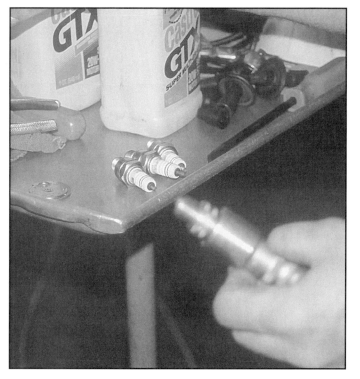

3. After making sure the plugs have the proper gap (0.026"), George put a tiny bit of anti-seize compound on the threads, then installed the plugs. The proper torque for the plugs is between 15 and 22 ft-lb.

4. George unscrews the end of the plug wires to make it easier to thread them through the 36 hp-only plug wire holder. He can also trim them to avoid any excess wire. If you are using your old wires over again, pay particular attention to the round rubber air dams at the end of the wire. If they are cracked, or don't seat against the cylinder tin anymore, they'll need to be replaced.

5. George then installs the points and condensor. A little tool called a "screw starter" is useful when putting the little point locking screw back down into the distributor.

6. With the distributor cam at its highest point, George sets the point gap at 0.016".

7. A little distributor cam lube is applied to the distributor cam, followed by a drop of oil on the felt piece in the top of the distributor shaft.

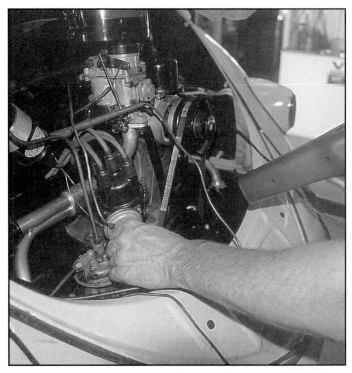

8. Using the stroboscopic timing light, the timing on this particular 36 hp unit is set 7.5 degrees before Top Dead Center.

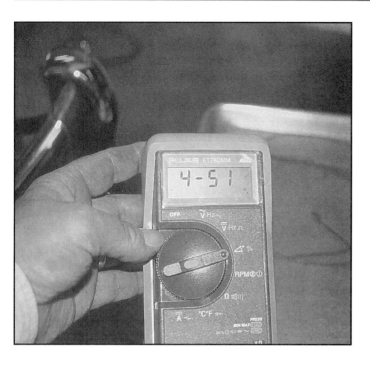

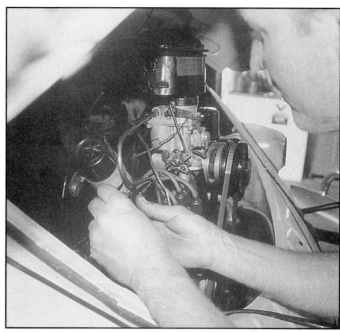

9. George also checked the dwell on the points. The book calls for 50 degrees and we had 51, so we left it alone.

10. The carburetor is adjusted next. Turn the screw on the distributor side of the carburetor until the engine starts to sputter and miss, then back the screw out until the engine is running its smoothest. George set the idle-speed screw to 550 rpm.

11. With the car warmed up, George raised the car up on a hoist, and while the oil was still warm and any particles of metal, fiber and dirt are still suspended in the oil, he drained it. One thing different about the 36 hp engine is that the oil strainer plate does not have a drain plug like some of the later model VW's. The drain plug is next to the strainer plate and screws directly in to the case. I recommend that you take the oil strainer out every oil change and clean it, because that is the only filter your oil has. With the oil mostly drained, George took the six 10mm nuts off the strainer plate and removes the first paper gasket, the strainer plate and the second gasket.

12. With everything clean and dry, George put on the first paper gasket, then the strainer, then the second paper gasket, then the strainer plate, followed by new copper washers and the nuts.

13. He put fresh oil (2.5 quarts) into the filler then checked the dipstick to make sure the crankcase was full.

14. On a car this old, there are only 10 grease fittings on the whole car; eight on the front end (the tie rods have been replaced, otherwise, if they were the originals, they might have grease fittings), and two back where the emergency brake cables exit the pan and go into a sleeve towards the rear brake backing plates. Give all these fittings a shot of grease or two.

FUEL PUMP REBUILD

20

Text & Photography by Dave Cormack

1. Here is the fuel pump we will be rebuilding. This pump already has one screw-in fitting, located on the intake, or suction, side. Begin by unscrewing this fitting, and, with a pair of pliers, pull out the other fitting by pulling and rotating it.

So you're driving down the road, and the old Beetle or Bus starts to cough and sputter, doesn't have any power, and finally shuts down. You pull over to the side of the road, lift up the decklid, and notice that you don't have any fuel in the fuel filter. "This can't be right," you say, "I just filled this &%#(~(%()! thing up!" Well, when was last time you checked out your fuel pump? It could just be that the diaphragm in the pump finally gave up the ghost. Disconnect the fuel line going into the carburetor, and let it hang. *Keep the ignition off*! or take the big wire off the center of the coil. Have a friend turn the engine over a few times while you are watching the fuel line. If you are by yourself, put the car in 3rd or 4th gear, and while keeping an eye on the fuel line, push the car ahead a few feet. If no gas comes out of the fuel line, you are either (1) out of gas, (2) have a plugged fuel line, or (3) your fuel pump just went away. If you can take the line going into the pump from the line that comes in to the engine compartment off and blow into it, and you can hear bubbles in the gas tank, then you don't have a plugged line, and you have fuel. Now, we're down to the fuel pump.

VW used a number of different pumps through the years, and some are rebuildable, and some aren't. If you have one of the old German pumps that has a small bolt right on the top, or if there are four screws holding the top of the pump on, you can use the fuel pump rebuild kit that we got from Wolfsburg West, in Anaheim, Calif. We also decided to do some fire-proofing while we were at it and install threaded fuel inlet pipes in the pump.

2. Remove the small bolt from the top of the pump, pull off the cover, and take out the screen. This is a fuel filter that many folks don't know they have. It wouldn't be a bad idea to clean this screen once in a while.

3. After scratching some line-up marks for re-assembly, remove the six screws that hold the pump body together, pull the two halves apart, exposing the diaphragm. This is the part that most commonly fails on these pumps.

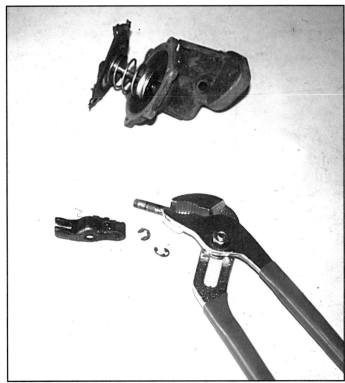

4. Remove the two small screws on the side of the pump, and the gasket. With a small screwdriver or similar instrument, remove the small circlip that holds the pivot pin in place. Drive out the pin.

5. Push down on the diaphragm and the operating lever can be pulled out, followed by the diaphragm itself. Don't lose the little spring inside the body of the pump.

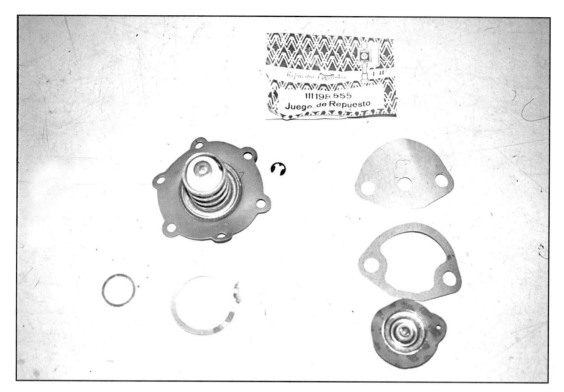

6. This is the rebuild kit from Wolfsburg West. If your pump had four screws on the top instead of one, you will be using the smaller gasket provided in the top of the pump. Also provided in the kit are the gaskets for the fuel pump stand, and now would be the time to replace it. They are cheap, and they can crack, creating an oily mess in your engine compartment.

7. & 8. Assemble in reverse order of taking it apart, using the lines you scratched into the pump to line up the inlet and outlet pipes. We used the tap and fittings from Pendergrass Tool to thread the outlet side of the pump, blow off the pump with compressed air, and, with a dab of Loctite®, we screwed the new fitting on.

9. We also drilled and tapped the inlet pipe on the top of the carburetor. Do this by removing the five screws that hold the top of the carb to the main body, and also the fuel line. Pull out the metal pipe just like you did on the fuel pump. Remove the needle and seat with a 14mm wrench, drill and tap, blow out the top of the carb with compressed air to make sure there are no metal shavings left. Reinstall the needle and seat.

10. Before installing the pump, push some grease into the cavity where the operating lever is and keep a little bit on the friction surface of the lever.

11. Here is the rebuilt pump, ready to install.

FRONT END & FRONT BRAKE UPGRADES

21

Text & Photography by Dave Cormack

1. The first thing to do is lift the front of the car up on jackstands. We had the luxury of using a hydraulic lift. It wouldn't be a bad idea, prior to jacking the car up, to take it down to your local car wash and rid the front end of the years of accumulated grease, grime, and filth that seems to attach itself to the front beam and link and king pins.

Although the focus of this book has been on restoration, the following chapter, as well as several others to come, deal with "restification" or "resto-custom." So, what constitutes a resto-custom? Most people would define it as this: A Beetle that retains the stock (or at least one outside color) paint scheme, an original style interior (no array of gauges on the dash here!), with a decent-sized, driveable engine/trans combination. Additionally, one of the most important aspects of a resto-custom is that it is lowered in the front and runs some type of aftermarket wheels. To begin, we will be putting on a lowered front end, upgrading the braking system, and installing the wheels and tires.

The base car is a 1957 Beetle that has the factory sunroof. It has been a daily driver for over 10 years. After that period of time, the front end was loosening, the engine was tired, and the trans was starting to whine. The brakes, being the original 1957 units with the two-bolt wheel cylinders, just weren't up to par for driving on the freeways of Southern California. The car is supposed to be driven a lot—rain or shine—to and from shows around the California area.

With this in mind, we went to Old Speed, in Paramount, Calif., and had a talk with Russell Ludwig, the owner. We decided to install a SoCal Imports lowered front beam, complete with a new TRW steering box, tie rods, spindles, etc. In fact, all we had to do was install the beam, set the toe-in, add the brakes to the front, and away we went. In the next chapter, we'll be upgrading the rear brakes, tires, and wheels as well.

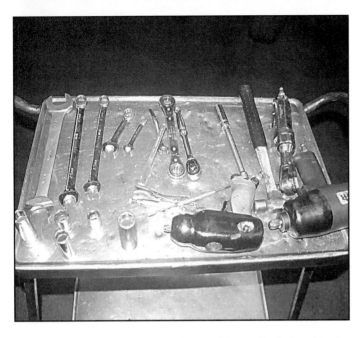

2. You can do this operation at home with your basic hand tools; however, Dave used an array of air powered tools to make life a little easier. About the only thing the average VW guy might not have would be an air powered "pickle fork" to separate the tie rod ends.

3. Now that the car is up in the air, remove the hub caps and the wheels.

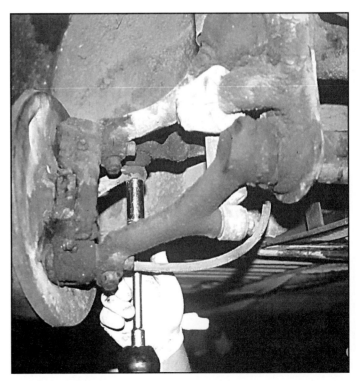

4. Take the clip or the cotter pin out of the driver's side brake drum center cap and withdraw the speedometer cable.

5. Remove the cotter pin on the long tie rod and remove the nut on the rod end.

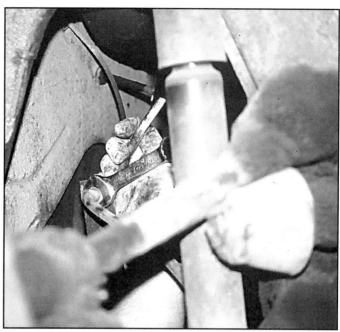

6. Remove the "U" shaped clamp on the frame that holds the brake line in place.

7. Separate the brake lines at this connection; be careful, don't mess up the threads or the head of the brake line.

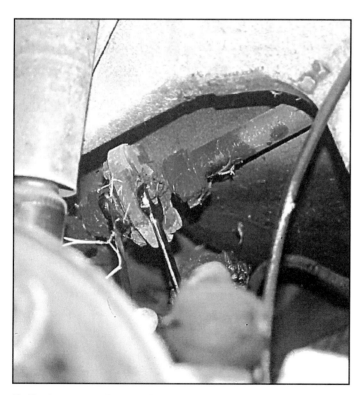

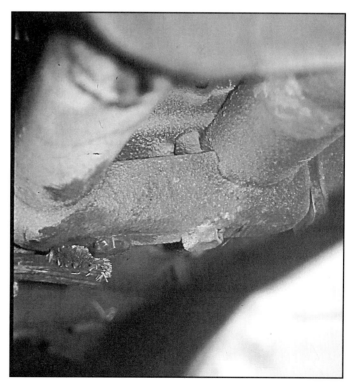

8. Next, remove the steering coupler. We used a new one from SoCal Imports, so this one will be thrown away.

9. There are four bolts that hold the beam to the frame head. I would suggest taking a wire brush to these, as they are always full of dirt and crud. Besides, it will make re-assembly that much easier.

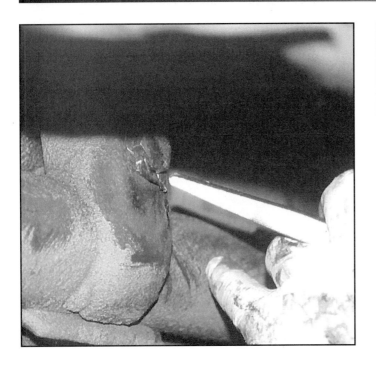
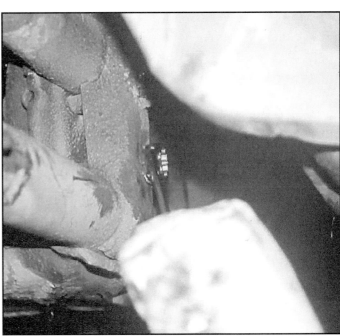

10. & 10a. There are locking tabs on the four bolts that need to be pried back before you can loosen the bolts.

11. & 11a. Since this is a 1957, it wasn't necessary to remove the gas tank; however, these two bolts, in front of the tank must be removed, along with the square washer and the rubber mount. On a 1960 and later, the tank should be pulled to access these two bolts.

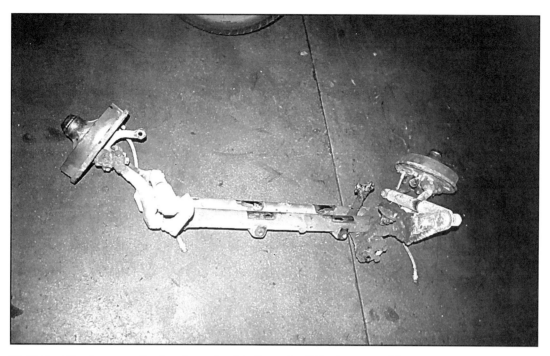

12. Grab a friend, remove the four frame head bolts, and pull the beam out. It's pretty heavy, so be careful. Here's what the old, original, 1957 front beam looked like after 40 years of use. Not too pretty. We used a later front end that incorporates a steering stabilizer.

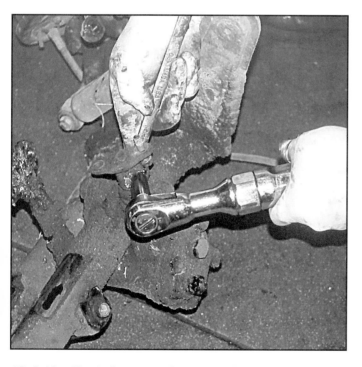

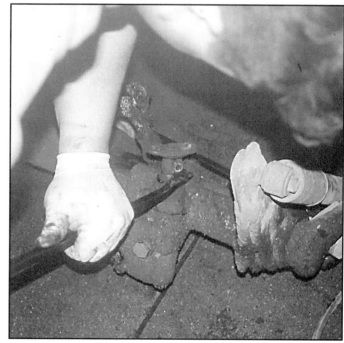

13. & 13a. About all we are going to use off the old beam is the coupler for the steering box. Take the nut out of the collar and pry the coupler off.

14. Here is the new beam from SoCal Imports. We decided to get the complete unit, with adjusters, so all the work was already done. We just had to bolt it in.

15. OK, I hope you didn't let your friend get too far away, because it's time to lift the new beam into place. Old Speed gets the beam up in place then hangs it from the top two bolts.

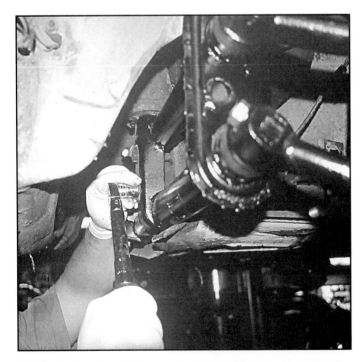

16. The bottom four bolts were torqued to 36 ft-lbs. After that, the lock tabs (you did remember them, didn't you?) were bent back over.

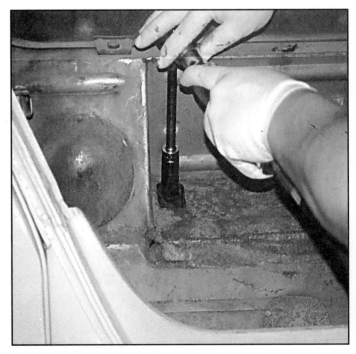

17. The top bolts were torqued to 14 ft-lbs.

18. Now we switched to the master cylinder installation. It is advisable to use a tubing, or flare, wrench on these fittings to avoid rounding the head off or twisting the metal brake line.

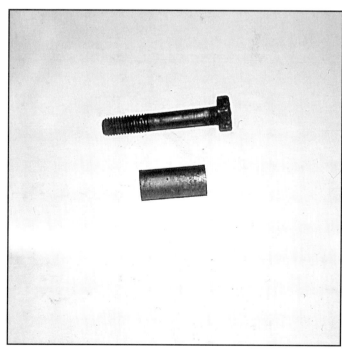

19. & 19a. There are two bolts holding the master cylinder in, along with a crush sleeve that goes through the firewall. You must use these crush sleeves; otherwise the firewall will flex when the brakes are applied.

20. We got a new reservoir plug from SoCal Imports; the old one had definitely seen better days.

21. Now the master cylinder can be put into place. Don't tighten the bolts and crush sleeve yet—leave them a little loose so it will be easier fitting the brake lines to the cylinder.

22. We also decided to upgrade to a new TRW steering box. These are available at a very little extra cost from SoCal when you order the beam. The new box comes full of oil so it is ready to install right out of the box.

23. Install the pitman arm. It will only go on one way, due to the teeth on it and the steering shaft.

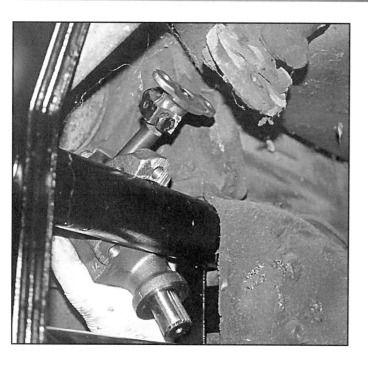

24. While you are at it, this would be the time to put the old coupler on the steering shaft.

25. We got the new rubber coupler from SoCal Imports. They are inexpensive, and since we were going "all the way," it seemed dumb to not get one.

26. Install the steering box, using the U-shaped clamp provided, but don't tighten it down just yet.

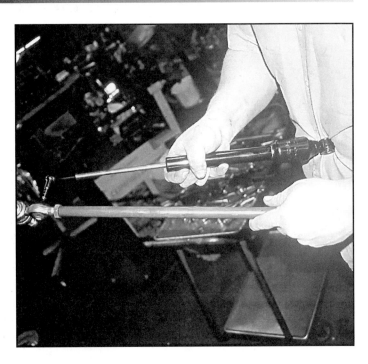

28. It's a good idea to put the steering stabilizer on before you install the long tie rod.

27. Install the shorter tie rod. Go ahead and tighten it down but leave the adjusters loose; we will need to use them when we adjust the toe-in.

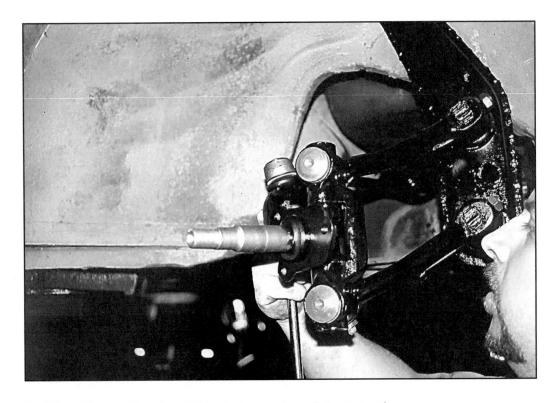

29. OK, put the long tie rod on, tighten it down and install the cotter pin.

30. Here is what we have up to this point. Looking good so far!

31. & 31a. We installed the lowered shocks from SoCal Imports. We began by applying a light coat of grease to the lower shock mount, and tightening it down. Do the same with the top shock bolt.

32. Since we decided to upgrade the front brakes to the less expensive, bigger, and more obtainable 1958-1964 front brakes, we had to change the backing plates.

33. The backing plates just bolted onto the spindle the way the old ones came off.

34. Grease all the areas on the backing plate that have the brake shoes rubbing on them.

35. Install the new SoCal Imports front wheel cylinders. It would, once again, be a good idea to leave them a little loose so it is easier to thread the brake hoses.

36. We safety wired the backing plate bolts, just like the factory did.

37. A little bit of grease on the brake shoe where it goes into the adjuster didn't hurt either.

38. & 38a. Now the shoes can be installed, followed by the locating pin, the spring, the "hat," that holds the shoe in place and the return springs.

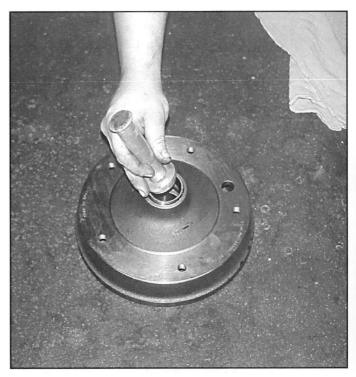

39. Now we are ready for the drum assembly. We installed the bearings and races first. Just to make sure, we put the drums on Old Speed's brake drum lathe and gave them a tiny clean up cut.

40. OK, we put the new inner and outer bearing races in. Refer to Chapter 10 for the ball-to-roller bearing conversion.

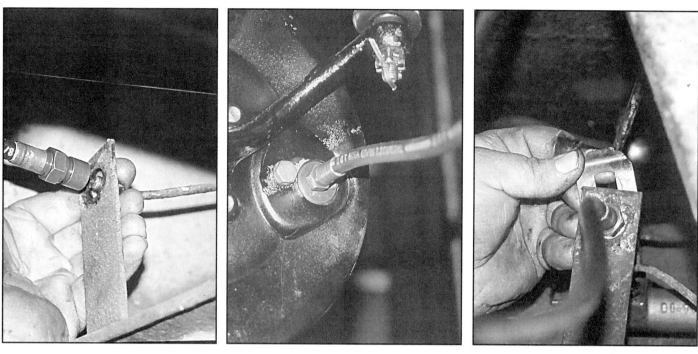

41., 41a. & 41b. We went ahead and put the new brake hoses on, leaving everything (except the U-shaped clamp) loose.

42. Here is the drum, ready for the bearings and seals.

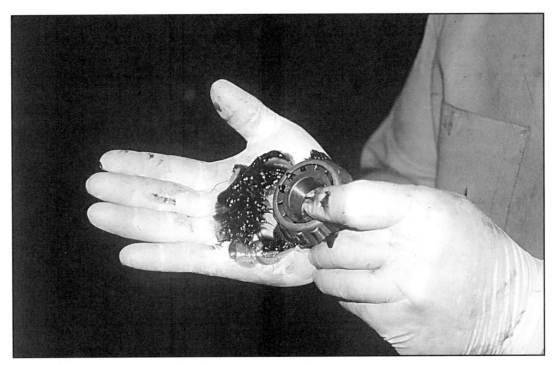

43. There are several different ways to pack the wheel bearings. Dave preferred to do it with the hand-pack method; the main thing is to get the grease all the way through the bearing.

44. & 44a. We took some emery paper and did the shoeshine routine to the spindle until the bearing slid off and on with relative ease. We then put the inner bearing in the drum, followed by the grease seal.

45. Install the drum, followed by the outer bearing and thrust washer.

46. Once again, refer to Chapter 10 for how to adjust the wheel bearings. Be sure you use a new locking tab washer, bent over so that the spindle nuts cannot come loose.

47. Reinstall the old tires and wheels for the time being.

48. With the car back on the ground, set the toe-in. Dave preferred to set the toe-in on a new front beam to 1/8-inch narrower in front than in the rear. Once you have the toe-in set, tighten up the lock nuts on the tie rods, and bend the locking tabs over.

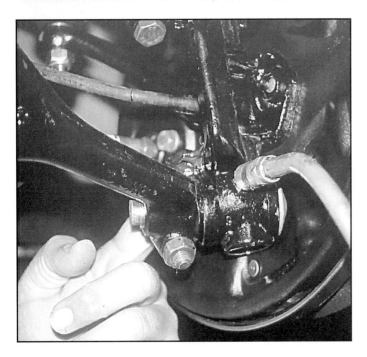

49. Now put the car back in the air and tighten everything—even the stuff you already tightened. Go over everything three or four times if you have to, just make sure everything is tight. Grease all the zerk fittings on the front end. If you have a link pin front end, as we do, you should have eight fittings. Find them all, and shoot the grease to them until you see it coming out of somewhere.

50. We put the new dust covers on, followed by the speedometer cable on the driver's side and the cotter key.

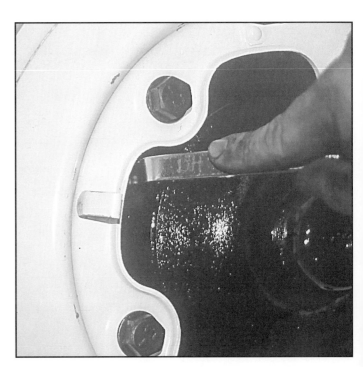

51. We adjusted the brake rod now, using the lock nuts to adjust the rod so that there is 1/8 to 1/4-inch play before the rod contacts the master cylinder.

52. Adjust the front brakes, and you are done with the front. We will finish up the suspension and braking modifications by installing the Type III brakes, and installing the wheels and tires in the next chapter.

UPGRADING THE REAR BRAKES

22

Text & Photography by Dave Cormack

1. First, remove the hubcap and take the cotter key out of the 36mm head brake drum nut. We will be using new ones from SoCal.

In Chapter 21, we installed a lowered front beam, a new steering box, and the later (1958–1964) front brakes on a 1957 Sunroof Beetle. So now the front is dropped and the brakes are new from the master cylinder forward; what about the rear brakes? As everyone knows, that's where the weight is in a Beetle, and the old skinny brakes could certainly be brought up to modern day standards.

Other features that set a resto-custom apart from a completely restored stock car are the wheels and tires; resto-customs often have little ones in front and big fat ones in the back. So in this chapter, we are going to install the biggest drum brakes we can get on the back, and install some Empi–style fully polished five-spoke

wheels, with big/little tires. We went back to Old Speed, in Paramount, Calif., to finish up these rear brake and suspension modifications, armed with more parts ordered from SoCal Imports, of Long Beach, Calif.

While we could have gone the handmade billet, custom-fabricated four-wheel disc brake route, we went with the most cost-effective way of improving the braking performance of our ride. About the only thing we had to modify was that we had to have Old Speed mill about a half inch of the snout of the Type III rear brake drums, in order to fit them on our narrow-axle trans.

2. These brake drum nuts are supposed to be torqued to 217 ft-lbs, so they can be a little tough to get loose. You might want to un-adjust your brakes to make it easier to get the drum off when the nut has been taken off.

3. The next thing to do is to take the brake line loose from the wheel cylinder. Sharp-eyed readers may notice that this car already has the 1958 to 1964 rear brakes, with the backing plates turned upside down to accommodate the parking brake cable. This will be fixed when we install the later Type III backing plates, by using the 1968-and-later parking brake cables.

4. Remove the rear axle bearing retainer. Loosen up the four bolts holding the backing plate on, and have a drain pan handy. If you had enough gear oil in your trans, it will begin to leak all over the floor unless you are prepared.

5. While holding on to the axle, pop the backing plate off. There is nothing here that we are going to reuse so either toss these items or save them for a future project.

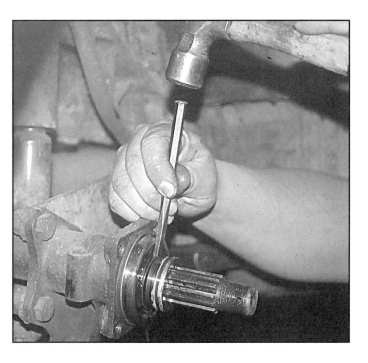

6. Dave uses a chisel with a few well-educated taps to remove the collar off the axle.

7. After cleaning the bearing retainer, Dave reinstalls the spacer washer, followed by a new rubber seal.

8. Reinstall the collar, with the bevel facing inwards, so you don't crush the O-ring.

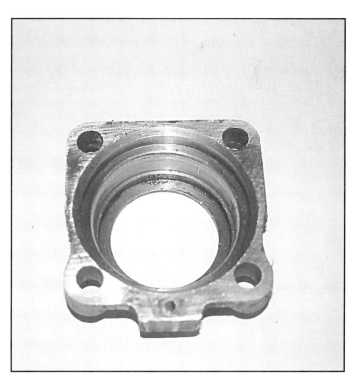

9. Check the surface of the bearing retainer. If it is not perfectly flat and a lot of them aren't (due to being taken off and on a thousand times), use a file or a piece of sandpaper on a flat surface to flatten the surface.

149

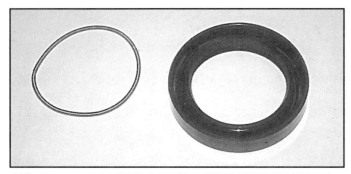

11. Clean the surface of the axle tube with carburetor cleaner, or whatever, just make sure that it is clean.

10. & 10a. Dave prefers to remove the little spring from the seal before using a 36 mm socket to drive the seal into the bearing retainer.

12., 12a. & 12b. Not taking any chances of a leak, Dave uses a little sealer on both sides of the gasket, followed by the new O-ring.

13. Put the backing plate on, making sure the holes for the parking brake cable are towards the front, and then install the bearing retainer, and torque the bolts to 43 ft.-lbs. On the gasket, make sure the little drain hole is pointed down, also. At this time, you will notice the backing plates are on upside down; that will be remedied on photo number 20. We did this because we used the old parking brake cables, which come in through the back of the backing plate, instead of the front, like the later style.

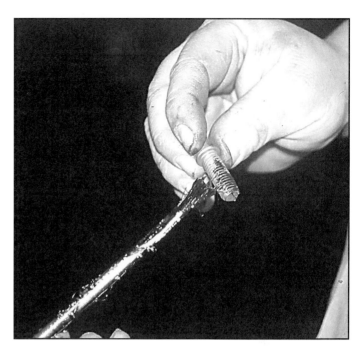

14. Put a little dab of grease on the friction surfaces of the adjusters to make sure we don't have any problems down the road with the adjusters freezing up.

15. Dave also puts a little grease on the friction surface of the backing plate.

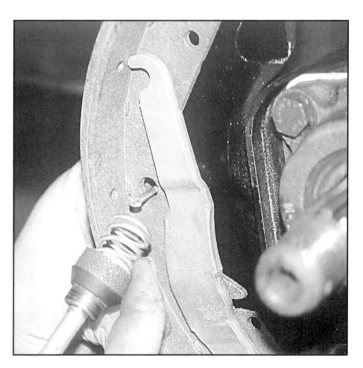

16. Now we are ready to install the brake shoes, the parking brake hardware, and the drums. We went ahead and got all-new brake hardware from SoCal, because the old stuff wasn't wide enough. Besides, why take a chance? We also turned the backing plates right side up, with the wheel cylinders at the top and used the 1968-and-later parking brake cables so everything would fit properly, and work like it should.

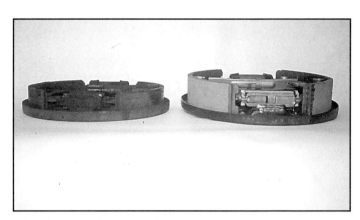

18. This comparison shot of the new vs. the old will demonstrate why we went with the Type III brakes in the rear. This car will be able to stop, that's for sure!

17. This is what the brake assembly should look like when all components are installed. Drums are next.

19. & 19a. The snout has to be milled down on these massive early Type III drums 0.525 of an inch to fit the narrow-axle trans. Notice that the snout is about 1/2 inch shorter on the one drum that is ready to go on. Old Speed also puts a slight bevel in the snout of the drum, so the next time the drum needs to go on a brake drum lathe for turning, it will be self–centering.

20. The drum goes on, along with the axle nut. Dave torques the nut to a minimum of 217 ft-lbs, and reinstalls a new cotter key.

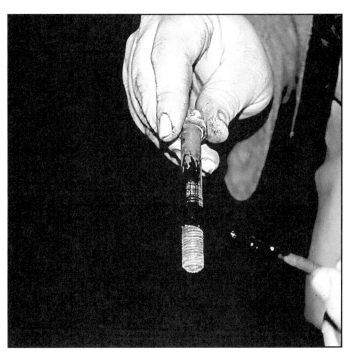

21. Dave bleeds the brakes, starting with the wheel cylinder farthest from the master cylinder—in this case the right rear cylinder. Bleed the cylinder until there is nothing but fresh, clean fluid coming out of the bleeder valve.

22. Dave greases the upper and lower shock bolt, prior to installing the KYB Gas-A-Just shocks in the rear.

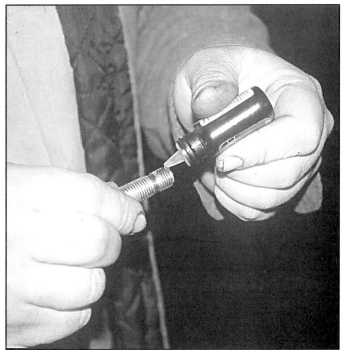

23. & 23a. Now, for the final touch—the installation of the polished Empi-style 5-spoke wheels, with the 195-65/15 Nankang tires in the back, and Nankang 145–15 tires in front. You will have to install studs into the drums to make these wheels fit. Don't worry, SoCal has them in stock, along with all of the other parts used. Before the studs are screwed into the brake drums, he puts a little dab of Loctite, or similar thread locker on the stud, to make sure the stud stays put. He then puts them in with an Allen wrench until they bottom out.

24. Here is the drum, all studded up and ready for the wheels and tires.

25. One thing we had to do was to grind the hub of the front brake drum just a little to make clearance for the wheel center caps. It's not much, but the caps wouldn't go on without it. The back wheels fit just fine, however.

These before and after shots illustrate the dramatic effect our "resto-custom" mods have made on the overall ride height, braking ability and look of our Beetle.

FLOORPAN REJUVENATION

Text & Photography by Dave Cormack

1. Here is the floorpan of the *VW Trends* / SoCal Imports Project: Mail Order Resto-Custom. Not bad, actually; at least we don't have any gaping holes, but we need to do something about the rust before it gets worse and makes a "Flintstone" car out of the project!

If you are lucky, and your Beetle has been carefully garaged, coated with undercoating, and fortunate to live in a dry climate, then the floorpan just may have survived with minimal damage. Some floorpans need nothing more than a good cleaning and removal of some surface rust periodically to keep them intact for decades. Fortunately, there are a number of sealers on the market that claim to stop surface rust from spreading. We decided to give one particular brand a try.

The idea is really simple: If you can prevent moisture from getting to the metal, then the rust cannot grow and spread. The produce we chose to use is POR-15 (POR for "Paint Over Rust"), by Restomotive Laboratories, in Morristown, N.J. POR-15 is fairly easy to use, as long as the directions supplied in their Floorpan and Trunk Restoration Kit are followed.

One thing about the POR-15 that separates it from other products is that most coatings deteriorate with exposure to moisture. POR-15, on the other hand, is actually strengthened by exposure to moisture, when properly applied. To test its strength, we have bounced around on the floorpan to try and weaken or crack this stuff. We even gave it a good sharp blow with a hammer (Note: This is *not* recommended!) and tried to get the stuff to flake, peel, or break, and could not do it. POR-15 chemically bonds to the rust and forms a rock-hard, non-porous coating that I couldn't chip, crack, or peel. After applying it with the brushes provided in the kit, you can paint, apply plastic filler, or put fiberglass over it; just about anything will bond to the POR–15. We even tried to sand it after it cured, just to see if it was as hard as they said it was. It was like sanding a rock. This stuff is pretty amazing in what it can do. We'll let you know in twenty years how it held up.

Resto-Motive also makes other products, including a gas tank sealer, engine enamels, a sealer for exhaust manifolds and mufflers that will withstand temperatures up to 2,000 degrees centigrade, and others. These products have been used in a wide variety of auto restorations, with very good results.

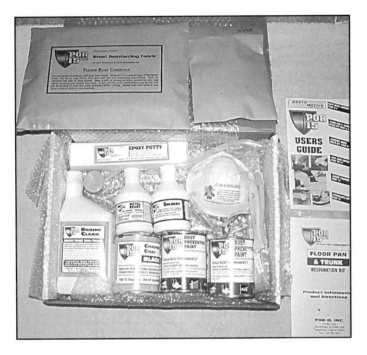

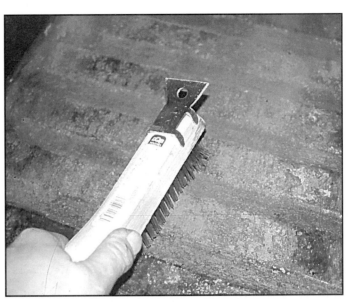

3. Begin the preparation by taking a wire brush and going over the surface to be coated, to remove any loose, scaly rust and any grease or contaminants that are present on the pan. Remember that Big Gulp you spilled last year? It's got to come out of there.

2. This is the Floorpan and Trunk Restoration Kit. It comes with everything you will need to rejuvenate your tired, rusty floorpan; it even has gloves, a respirator and brushes. Make sure you use the safety equipment provided with the kit—this stuff gives off some fairly unpleasant fumes when it is curing, and if you get it on your hands, nothing, except time, will remove it.

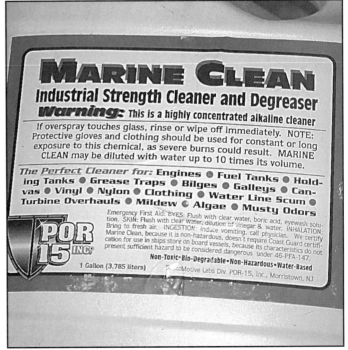

4. Now that the rust, scale and grease are loose, vacuum thoroughly.

5. Wash the area you just wire-brushed and vacuumed with the Marine Clean, provided in the kit, mixed with some hot water. Rinse thoroughly.

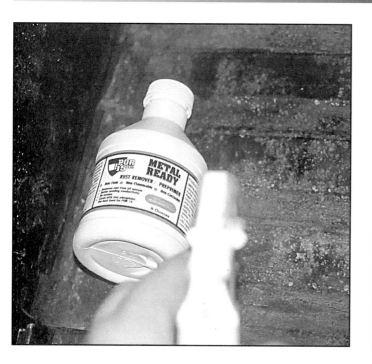

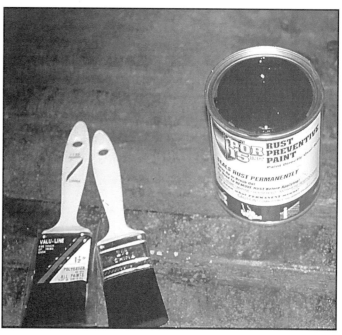

6. Now, begin to spray the pan with POR–15 Metal-Ready. It is important to keep the area wet with Metal Ready for 20 to 30 minutes. Heavier rust deposits may take a little longer. The Metal Ready leaves a coat of zinc phosphate, which is a perfect primer for the next step. If you are getting ready to treat clean, unrusted metal, use some Marine Clean (also provided), before the Metal-Ready. This will remove any oil or residue left by the mill when the metal was shipped.

7. Before you proceed to the next step, make sure the area is completely dry. It is best to wait overnight or use a hair dryer to make sure that the metal is totally dry.

8. Using the brushes provided with the kit, apply the POR–15 Rust Preventitive Paint.

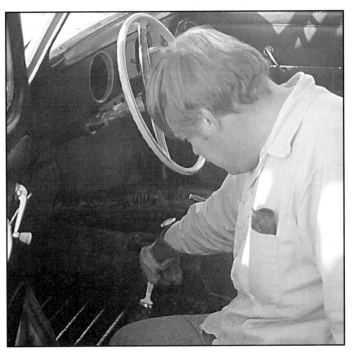

9. If you have some holes that need to be filled, follow the directions given to apply the steel reinforcing fabric and the POR-5 Silver. I was lucky; my pan was still in good shape, so I was able to skip this step. Also, I was able to escape using the Epoxy Putty, also supplied, to fill in any low areas. I have seen this stuff used before, and believe me, it works. You can take a rusty, swiss-cheese looking pan, and make it look almost new, with a little time and effort. I tried this stuff later on the floors of my 1961 Single Cab, as you can tell by the photos, and it worked.

10. Now we move on to the Topcoat of the Chassis Coat Black. It just brushes on, like the POR–15 Silver. Make sure you get into all the nooks and crannies to completely seal the area, or rust will find its way back in and defeat what you are trying to do.

11. Okay, after the curing time, this is what we have. Looks a little different, yes? If the finished product will have continuous exposure to ultra-violet rays you should topcoat it with the Chassis Coat Black. It won't hurt the POR-15 to be exposed, however, but it will change appearance over the years.

REPLACING SHOCKS

24

Text & Photography by D.E. Meyer

1. Remove the hub caps and use the 19mm socket and breaker bar to loosen the lug nuts. Raise the car with floorjack placed under the stock jack location, and set the car on jack stands.

The lowly shock absorbers must be the most forgotten parts on a car, or at least the most taken for granted. Shocks are typically less than the best when they come from the factory, and only then they do an adequate job. Shock absorbers do have their limits, though. If neglected long enough, they can eventually spit out the little rubber bushing at the mounting points and then rattle metal-to-metal over every bump until you finally become agitated enough to replace them. When you finally do, you will kick yourself for not having done so sooner. The improvement is so noticeable that it is safe to say that every car would benefit from the installation of new shocks.

When it comes to selecting a shock, one misconception that many people have is that stiffer is always better. Our requirements sent us in search of a shock with good control, but one that still allowed full the suspension travel.

Our 1961 Beetle's shocks were shot. This Bug is driven down a rutted, washed-out, mile-long dirt road every day. The shocks had jettisoned the rubber bushings long ago, and the constant bone-rattling ride was a sign that it was time for action. We decided that a set of KYB GR2 shocks would be perfect for our needs. These shocks are relatively inexpensive, and prove that the most costly shock is not necessarily the best one. The shocks bolted on very quickly and easily, and the improved performance and ride made us wonder why we ever hesitated to put them on sooner.

2. Use a 17mm wrench to remove the top shock bolt. It threads into the top of the shock tower. You may need to use a little leverage to break it loose. Next, remove the bottom nut. The bottom is a stud that is part of the spindle. Pull the shock off.

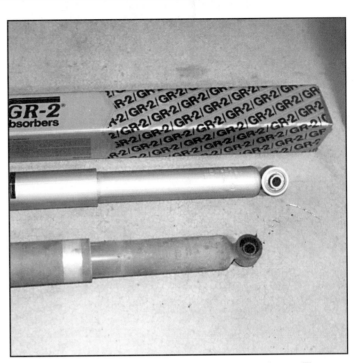

3. Check out the difference between the old and new. The new GR2s are not the wrong size; they have pressure to keep them extended. The source of all that clanking coming from the front end was the lack of a rubber bushing between the metal bushing and the shock eye.

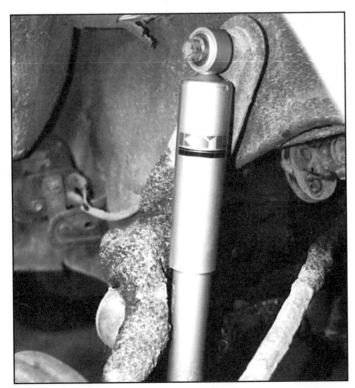

4. To install the new shock, just reverse the removal procedure.

5. The rear shock installs much the same as the front, with the exception of being connected to the mount with a complete bolt and nut. What this means is that you will need a pair of wrenches to remove and tighten the shock bolts in the rear.

SPLIT WINDOW ERA ACCESSORIES 25

by Lee Thomas Hedges

A new 1953 Export model Beetle Sedan (nicknamed the Zwitter Split) stands proud with the addition of dual front fog lights and chromed dual Hella "city" horns mounted to the front bumper. The Zwitter Split was a cross-over model of early 1953 that mated the split rear window with a new Oval Window era dash layout. These are one of the most desirable Splits since they have the most modern mechanical features with the original split rear window.

The Volkswagenwerk factory changed hands in 1948, from previous post-war British Occupation control into German control at the hands of their legendary leader, Heinz Nordhoff. Nordhoff had many plans for the Volkswagen, one of which was to expand its sales outside of Germany into Europe and North America. The first Export model Sedans were available in 1949, alongside the introduction of the Beetle Cabriolet. The Export model Beetles were considered "deluxe" versions and were fitted with extras including aluminum body trim, chromed bumpers and lights, as well as more comfortable interior accommodations. Although Volkswagen equipped its cars with everything necessary for safe and comfortable driving, and its design was practical and pleasing to the eye, some VW owners desired additional accessories. Happy to comply with the public demand, the factory designed many interesting accessories for these early VW "Split Window" models built from 1949–53.

Most of the accessories offered by the VW factory were designed to make the car more comfortable and fun to drive. These items included radios, folding seats into beds, interior fans, ashtrays, and passenger headrests. Some accessories were designed to make the car safer when driving in all conditions. These items included fog lights, extra-loud horns, steering wheel locks, additional brake lights, reverse warning lights, tool kits, and locking dual glovebox doors. Then, of course, there were the accessories that simply made the Beetle look better. These included aluminum exhaust tips, wheel trim rings, under-dash parcel trays, and even rear seat storage areas.

Perhaps the largest supplier of "Split Window" era accessories for the Volkswagen was a company called Kamei. They specialized in accessories for German vehicles, and with Volkswagen's tremendous success in the early 1950s, Kamei predicted that the small car market would be huge. Kamei continued supplying accessories to VW owners through the 1960s and became a renowned worldwide supplier. One of the strangest accessories for the early Beetles was a front air dam that replaced the front bumper and was designed to increase the aerodynamic flow of the Beetle. With a standard 25-horsepower engine that put out 1100cc, any help in the speed department was a blessing to those owners that desired a bit more from their new Beetles.

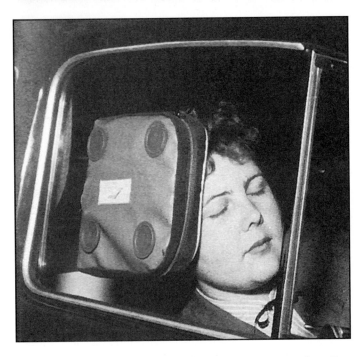

Here's a rarest of the rare for your Split Window; a Kamei suction cup padded pillow for the passenger.

This 1950 Split features an aluminum flared single exhaust tip, designed to beautify the rear end.

Here's a close-up of the 1950 Split dash showcasing the very rare steering wheel lock with original keys. Notice the cigar lighter on the lower right and the round ash tray.

(Above) This early photo of a 1950 Split features a great deal of highly collectible accessories to make this lady's drive more enjoyable. Check out the under-dash radio with built-in speaker underneath and the round dash clock opposite the speedometer. If you look closely you can see the round ivory cigar lighter (near her hand) and the round ivory pull-out ash tray just above the lighter.

(Right) Something that most Split owners needed to avoid boredom during the long drives on the German autobahn was this Telefunken "all Europe" radio. It was designed to fill the right side dash pod instead of the clock or round ash tray. The black-faced speedometer pod was used in 1949 and can easily be identified by the white VW logo at the top of the gauge.

All of the Split Window Beetles had only one brake light which was housed in the "pope's nose" license plate housing. This 1950 Split Sedan features dual brake lights in thin units above the round reflectors as well as a left-side reverse light mounted to the bumper.

Another interesting radio for the Splits was this Loewe model. Like the Telefunken, it features a speaker grill in the center, but the Loewe has the European city selections located on the outside tuning ring. Some of the cities include London, Prague, Florence, Moskow, Paris and Oslo.

To add comfort to the drive, this Split dash features an accessory electric fan & large round ash tray located in the right-side dash pod.

This 1952 Standard model Beetle features the ever-popular headlight eyebrows made of chromed brass, designed to concentrate the weak 6 Volt headlight beam reflection back down onto the pavement for additional visibility.

Another nice Kamei accessory item from their 1952 catalog is this useful backseat storage compartment, color coordinated with the matching accessory seat upholstery.

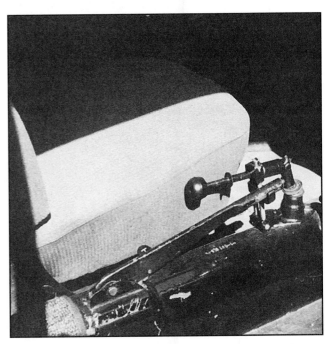

This special gear shift arm from a 1950 Beetle was designed to fold backward and lay flat when the passengers needed more space.

This unique (and confounding) accelerator pedal accessory is from the 1951 Kamei catalog, and was possibly designed for a right-foot amputee, foot rest or dual pedal controls. Can you figure it out?

Perhaps the strangest and rarest early Split accessory is this 1952 Kamei spoiler. Designed for enhanced aerodynamics, it replaced the front bumper but mounted to the original bumper brackets.

A PRISTINE 1954 BEETLE

by Ryan Lee Price
Photos by Rob Hallstrom

Though he is retired from the classroom, mathematics professor Paul Cochrane has traded in his teacher's editions for VW shop manuals, and instead of making his students stay after school and clap erasers, he just takes out their engines and sticks them in the corner of the garage. Meet one of his students: a bright '54 that climbed to the head of the class. Of course, the road to graduation was a rocky path, but with Cochrane's patience and attention to detail, the well-rounded pupil soon became the teacher's pet.

Paul is like most Volkswagen enthusiasts: The first car he ever owned was a Volkswagen, a 1960 Ragtop he bought in 1966. "I loved the car. I dated my wife in that car and she loved it. It was wonderful to drive at night, push

back the canvas sunroof and drive under the stars. I sold it after a year and wished many times that I had not done so." Since then, Paul has owned many Volkswagens, but the purchase of his current pride and joy happened partly part by accident and mostly by luck.

In the spring of 1996, Paul and his wife, Donna, attended a show in Manassas—"a raining and miserable show,"—when Donna struck up a casual conversation with a man who had a 1954 Beetle. The Virginia man was only looking to get back his original investment of $5000 when he agreed to sell it. "The price seemed high at the time," admitted Cochrane, "but after seeing it, the car looked solid, and it had an original tool kit and a spare gas can," which he figured were worth at least a $1000 by itself.

Unfortunately, while the Cochranes were weighing the pros and cons, someone else had stepped in and started negotiating for the car, even taking it for a test drive. Thinking the car was sold, they gave up, only to discover later that the person who test drove it didn't put any money down. "We sent a check immediately to clinch the deal," remembered Cochrane.

Not sure how the car would fare on the trip from Alexandria, Virginia, to its new home in Bloomsburg, Pennsylvania, a five-hour trip, the Cochranes decided it was best to tow the car home. But when a problem cropped up with the tow car, there was no alternative but to take a chance and drive the Beetle. Much to their surprise, the vehicle made the trip with no problems, even maintaining an average speed of around 55 mph.

When the car was safe at home, an inspection revealed that it needed a lot of attention. First and foremost, the well-worn tires were replaced with 5.60x15 Firestones from Coker's, and the body was painted a metallic Mercedes blue. The engine was filthy and completely incorrect. "It was a wonder we ever made a successful trip from Virginia," said Paul. The distributor rotor was from a later VW, and two gaskets had been put on

the engine side of the fuel pump with none on the other side. The carburetor's center shaft was broken and was patched with a piece of plastic tubing. The upholstery was a bright red and the carpet a shoddy gray.

"Otherwise," added Paul. "The car was solid and had the original pans." But much work had to be done.

After stripping off all of the broken parts, like the rusted-through spare tire well, Paul detailed and painted the original engine, fixing all of the leaks and replacing the carburetor. With information about the correct colors from the oval handbook from Ovals Only, "I ordered a new tan vinyl upholstery kit and door panels from BFY and was pleasantly surprised with the quality of kit I received." Dressler's Upholstery in Cocolamus, Pennyslvania, installed the blue-gray headliner, and a tan German square weave carpet kit was ordered from Dave Lometta.

Most of the major undercarriage work was done just in the last year. Paul pulled the entire front end, stripped the axle, steering box, drums and tie rods and painted everything a satin black.

Then he did the same to the rear end. Simultaneously, he disassembled the brakes, master cylinder, lines, etc. and detailed them. He sanded and repainted the pans, removing and replacing all of the pan bolts, detailing all of the channels.

But Paul Cochrane was still not satisfied.

"The car looked good in Mercedes blue and people loved the car at the shows we went to, but I was not pleased with the fact that it was not original." Contacting Kunkle Brothers in Selinsgrove, Pennsylvania, Paul asked them to repaint the car and do any of the necessary bodywork. At that time, he had the rear apron of a '56 modified and installed (for the H-patterned rear apron of a '54 could not be located). While at Kunkle Brothers, they resprayed the car with many coats of Strato Silver Metallic Blue acrylic enamel (L227) and then clear coated it—just like it was off of the assembly line. Also, the wheels were two-toned with Pearl White (L87) in the center and the Silver Metallic Blue around the outside.

To achieve the vintage look the Cochranes were longing for, they started to accessorize. First, they

rummaged through the boxes of extra parts that were included in the deal and found a Koch steering wheel, the tool kit, an AM/FM short-wave radio, heart taillights and European lenses for the front headlights. Then, Paul located a Motometer and had it installed and wired correctly, using a hand-drawn blueprint from a friend's Motometer. Finally, to top it all off, a BeKowa luggage rack finished the project. However, as restoration enthusiasts know, a project car is never completed: Still on the waiting list to be added is a Judson supercharger, which is currently being completely refurbished by George Folchi in Milford, Connecticut.

In addition to the '54, the Cochrane family includes a '65 and '67 Convertible, a '65 Karmann Ghia Convertible and a '97 Jetta. It is obvious that a lot of work and time was invested to make the '54 what it is today, clearly the main reason why it's this teacher's "pet."

Volkswagen Models...
Past, Present & Future

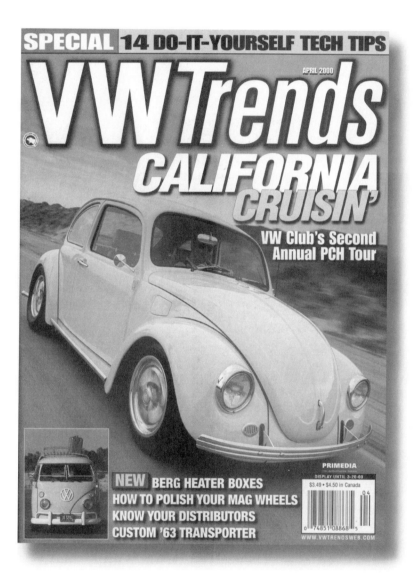